Psychology

Psychology

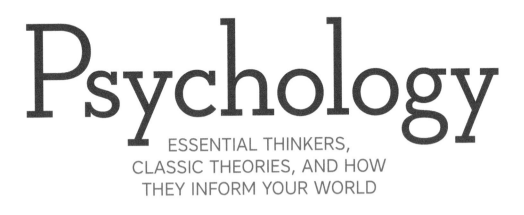

ESSENTIAL THINKERS,
CLASSIC THEORIES, AND HOW
THEY INFORM YOUR WORLD

Andrea Bonior, Ph.D.

Illustrations by Alex Westgate

ZEPHYROS
PRESS

To Andy
and Vance, Alina, and Ruby
who light up my brain

Contents

Introduction

Jean-Paul Sartre, in his play *No Exit*, wrote that hell is other people. That thought seems true enough when it brings to mind an overbooked cruise ship. But other people can populate heaven, too. Other people add depth to the world, whether their presence is linked to our highs or to our lows, to our most soaring joy or to our most confounding, miserable pain. Other people matter a great deal, and yet all of us can be such mysteries to each other.

What makes one person think one thing while another person thinks something else altogether? What causes our deepest and seemingly most unpredictable emotions? What is the difference between the brain and the mind, and between the mind and the body? What, really, are memories? What is love? How do our senses decode and make meaning of the thousands of sights, sounds, smells, and tastes we encounter each day? What does it mean to be conscious, and why do we often act in ways that don't make sense for our self-interest? What matters more—our DNA or our environment?

Psychology aims to answer all these questions, among countless others. In fact, some of these questions are at the very root of what we will ultimately come to make of our lives, of how we will find meaning, and of what we will view as our most important moments and relationships. Why we are who we are, and why we do what we do—these questions are fundamental to being human, and psychology offers us tools for finding answers.

If my shelves full of psychology texts are any indication, there are hundreds of theorists, researchers, and writers who deserve a place in psychology's Hall of Fame, and it pains me to leave so many of them out of this book. But what you'll find summarized here is the canon, a careful selection of those famous and infamous thinkers who best represent the field, and whose lifework tells us something particularly important about how our minds operate.

Whether you took a single introductory psychology course in school or majored in the subject, you may be looking for a refresher that can make psychology relevant to your daily life again and remind you of the theorists who inspired all those late-night conversations about the meaning of life (and about whether your roommate might be a narcissist). Even if you have no idea what psychology is all about, you may be interested in knowing what it is that makes you and other people behave the way you do. Whatever your background, if you'd like to understand more about yourself and the people around you, and about how psychology's biggest ideas and greatest breakthroughs are reflected in how we all live our lives, this is the book for you.

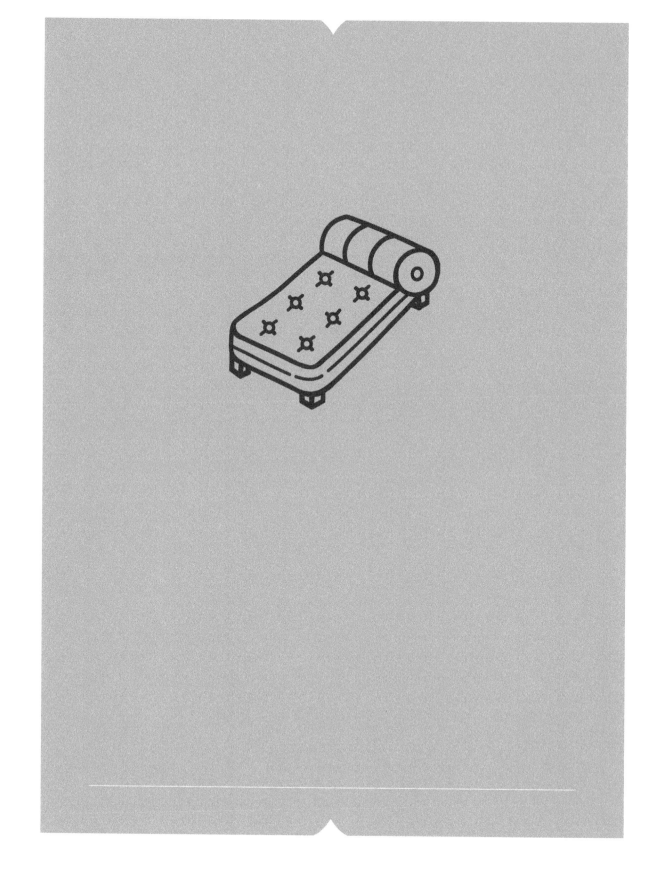

PART ONE

The Canon

Biological Psychology 12

Behavioral Psychology 30

Psychotherapy 51

Cognitive Psychology 90

Developmental Psychology 109

Psychology of Personality 137

Social Psychology 155

Timeline

C. 400 BCE Hippocrates and other figures of ancient Greece theorize about the four humors

1247 The Priory of St. Mary of Bethlehem (later "Bethlem" and "Bedlam"), one of the earliest official psychiatric hospitals, opens in London

C. 1440 Johannes Gutenberg invents the printing press

1647 René Descartes writes *The Description of the Human Body*

C. 1808 Franz Josef Gall pioneers phrenology, a practice based on the belief that the size and shape of the skull tell something about individual psychological characteristics

1859 Charles Darwin publishes *On the Origin of Species*

1861 Paul Broca identifies an area of the frontal lobe associated with language production

1879 Wilhelm Wundt establishes the first official psychology laboratory

1886 Sigmund Freud begins his clinical work in Vienna

1890 William James publishes *Principles of Psychology*

1898 Edward Thorndike develops the law of effect

1905 Alfred Binet creates his first intelligence test

1906 Ivan Pavlov publishes his first studies on classical conditioning

1911 Alfred Adler breaks away from Freud and forms his own school of psychotherapy

1913 John B. Watson publishes "Psychology as the Behaviorist Views It" in *Psychology Review* after its presentation as a lecture at Columbia University

1937 Karen Horney publishes *The Neurotic Personality of Our Time*

1950 Erik Erikson publishes *Childhood and Society*

1952 The first edition of the *Diagnostic and Statistical Manual of Mental Disorders* (*DSM*) is published

1956 Leon Festinger establishes the theory of cognitive dissonance

1961 Carl Rogers publishes *On Becoming a Person*

1963 Stanley Milgram publishes his first experiments on obedience to authority figures

1971 Elliot Aronson pioneers the jigsaw classroom

1971 Philip Zimbardo conducts the Stanford Prison Experiment

1976 Ulric Neisser publishes *Cognition and Reality*

1990 Elizabeth Loftus begins investigating the development of false memories

1997 Albert Bandura publishes *Self-Efficacy: The Exercise of Control*, which encapsulates decades of work

2006 Carol Dweck publishes *Mindset: The New Psychology of Success*

Biological Psychology

Biological psychology examines the intersection between the physical body, on the one hand, and emotional and cognitive reality, on the other. We might ask whether the early biological psychologists were ahead of their time. You might think so—turn on any television today, and you're bombarded with commercials promising that a pill-induced alteration in body chemistry is all it will take to fundamentally change your life. Exaggerated medical claims aside, though, we do know that biology influences behavior in remarkable ways, and that probably no two brains are alike. The ways in which any two brains can differ are innumerable, from the size of the lobes to the intensity of the various neurotransmitters' activity. But to what extent, exactly, do the brain's physical qualities matter when it comes to individual differences?

It was also biological psychology that began to grapple with the concept of heritability. Some of what makes you the person you are today may have been determined, at least in part, before you were born. But if your genetic makeup came from your parents, they probably also influenced your personality and your habits in myriad additional ways—no doubt you learned some of your typical attitudes and behavior simply by observing your parents as you grew up, and all that influence took place by way of your brain.

The brain is just one organ, but no other human organ comes close to the brain's complexity or plays such a fundamental role in shaping human identity.

As a rule, influential people in the field of biological psychology have been most concerned with understanding whether and how the anatomy and physiology of the human brain are directly correlated with human thought, emotion, and action.

René Descartes

BORN 1596, La Haye en Touraine, Kingdom of France

DIED 1650, Stockholm, Sweden

Educated at the University of Poitiers

BIG IDEA

René Descartes, whose fame is not primarily associated with psychology, made notable contributions to philosophy and mathematics. But his years of philosophizing on the nature of the mind, the scientific process, and the structures and mechanisms of the body's actions had an indelible impact on how we think about thinking itself. Descartes is known as the originator of a thoroughly modern concept—the **mind-body problem**, or the question of what the mind and the body are, and of how they interact.

Cogito ergo sum—"I think, therefore I am," a quote famous enough to be parodied on modern-day T-shirts—encompasses this towering figure's most famous theory. That theory says this: We must abandon our thoughts about anything that can be doubted because that thing, whatever it is, is fundamentally uncertain. According to Descartes, if we were to start again from scratch, making no assumptions that could be doubted, then we would be left with just one thing—the ability to doubt. And, for Descartes, it is our very ability to doubt, and to think, that makes us conscious and true beings.

This way of thinking is probably little more than an intellectual exercise that Descartes conducted within his own mind, but it's not hard to see its implications for the scientific method. Indeed, stripping away all assumptions before beginning an experiment is now something we see as a fundamental element of research.

Descartes is also credited with having advanced the notion of reflexes, even if certain aspects of his theory have long since been debunked and discarded. He believed that external stimuli could set off a series of events within the nerve cells that in turn would trigger the movement of what he called *animal spirits*. That part isn't true, of course, but Descartes was correct—and advanced—in thinking that the body responds in automatic ways to certain external stimuli. He further posited that the interaction between awareness and bodily responses—an interaction considered to be the essence of consciousness—occurs in the brain, within the pineal gland. Descartes understood this interaction to be a two-way phenomenon, with the body influencing the mind by making the mind aware of bodily reflexes, and with the mind in turn affecting the body by initiating movement. This notion of mutual influence is at the heart of dualism, the philosophical concept of mind and body as distinct entities.

If you were to follow this idea, you would go on to assume that the mind is not physically quantifiable—that it is without concrete substance, and that thoughts have no material quality. This conceptualization of the mind also encompasses our modern definition of the soul, since Descartes believed that the mind

survives bodily death. And the body, for its part, is limited and defined, according to Descartes—a physical substance through and through. This idea has a certain correspondence with the notion of primary qualities, as opposed to secondary qualities: Primary qualities—objective, observable, measurable characteristics—can be perceived apart from all subjectivity, whereas secondary qualities are not as concretely discernible and are therefore subject to bias, and to all the skewed interpretations that play a part in human perception. Similarly, Descartes distinguished between innate ideas, which he saw as springing up naturally, rather than through interaction with the outside world, and derived ideas, which he saw as born of direct external experience and of the memories formed from experience.

Notwithstanding Descartes's rather striking thoughts about animal spirits, he believed, notably, that the pineal gland is present only in human beings, and that only human beings possess real consciousness, the ability to reason, and the capacity to feel pain. As it happens, though, the pineal gland was first discovered in an ox, and various studies have demonstrated problem-solving abilities in animals as well as the presence of painful sensations in nonhuman mammals.

THEN WHAT?

The philosophy of Descartes—Cartesian philosophy, as it's called—had a direct impact on later research into human

sensation, thought, and experience. But some later theorists rejected the Cartesian conceptualization of dualism, holding instead that all experiences and things should be categorized in only one of two ways, as either material or immaterial. Thomas Hobbes understood mental processes to be caused by physical activity within the brain, and he believed that all knowledge arises from sensation; the Hobbesian view was that there are no innate ideas and everything is material. John Locke, although greatly influenced by Descartes's mechanistic approach, rejected Cartesian dualism in favor of empiricism. Along these lines, George

Berkeley (pronounced "Barkley") and Baruch Spinoza joined Hobbes and Locke in rejecting Cartesian ideas, but discussion of the mind-body problem continues to this day.

WHAT ABOUT ME?

The question of where the mind ends and the body begins, and vice versa, gained major traction with Cartesian philosophy, but of course this issue has yet to be definitively settled. We know that the mind affects the body and the body affects the mind, but at what point are they distinct entities? Is the material world real if our mind is not there to perceive it?

Some of the quirkiest party tricks are, at heart, explorations of the distinction that becomes evident between the mind and the body as reflexes overtake conscious thought. Try this: Sit with your right leg raised a few inches off the floor. Move your leg rhythmically in a circle, in a *clockwise* direction (that part's important.) Now, as you're doing that, raise your right index finger, and trace the number 6 in the air in front of you. Notice anything interesting about your right foot? It has almost certainly stopped moving clockwise, and it has probably begun to go in the opposite direction! You might ask what that foot is thinking, but this is a case of your conscious mind's woeful inability to triumph over your body's desperate, reflexive impulse to have both the right foot and the right finger moving in the same direction. That reflexive impulse dominates because your right foot and your right finger are both controlled by the left side, or hemisphere, of your brain, and your brain is trying to simplify things. Can you blame it? Now repeat the experiment, again moving your right leg in a clockwise circle, but this time use your left hand to trace the number 6 in the air. Now you shouldn't

see the same reflex. That's because the two different hemispheres of your brain can work concurrently on different tasks.

Reflexes certainly do matter. Sometimes the body reacts, and the mind has trouble overriding the body, no matter what the mind's intentions may be. We see this phenomenon when we sneeze, flinch, blink, recoil from a hot stove top, or freeze up in terror. We can thank René Descartes for being an early proponent of the notion of reflexes and for offering descriptions that have sparked study for centuries.

You may also be thinking in Cartesian terms if you're someone who ponders the nature of the soul or the qualities of God. Some clergymen who were contemporaries of Descartes believed that his works were subversive, even heretical, but he actually had a deep religious faith. His concept that the soul and the mind are one entity, and that they transcend the material world's constraints of time and space, is certainly one that millions of people still follow or at least think about. Is there something in the brain that rises above its physical nature, and that gives our personhood meaning beyond the trappings of this Earth? Descartes certainly thought so, but perhaps none of us can know for sure.

Charles Darwin

—•—

BORN 1809, Kent, England

DIED 1882, Shropshire, England

Educated at the University of
Edinburgh and Cambridge University

BIG IDEA

Charles Darwin's ideas fundamentally
and permanently altered the course of
psychology. No doubt you've heard of
Darwin, the father of evolutionary theory,
if only because of the Darwin Awards, a
tongue-in-cheek recognition of people who
improve the human gene pool by accidentally sterilizing or killing themselves
through their own unintelligent actions.
Darwin's name is invoked in this connection because of its association with the
notion of the survival of the fittest.

Darwin's seminal work, *On the Origin
of Species,* was published in 1859, and it
laid out his groundbreaking ideas on
natural selection and **sexual selection.** (Interestingly enough, Darwin's
insights preceded this book's publication
by many years, a fact that has led some to
believe that he was nervous about the
possibility that his work would have a
far-reaching negative impact on society.)
The term *natural selection* points to the
idea that nature, over time, will eliminate
maladaptive traits that are not useful to a
species, since specimens that have such
traits die off more quickly than their
counterparts that lack those traits. The
term *sexual selection* points to a more
active and intentional pursuit of various
adaptive traits as one aspect of mating
behavior. (In other words, Darwin believed
that organisms are capable of swiping

right, the way human beings do on apps like Tinder.) As for why sexual selection works, it's because potential mates who possess the adaptive traits are deemed more desirable: they're likely to survive longer and can propagate stronger members of the species because their adaptive traits will live on in their descendants. This process takes place at the level of the individual organism, of course, but it also has macro-level effects on the whole species.

Charles Darwin, following this logic, also surmised that many different species, including humans and apes, probably had a common ancestor. In other words, evolutionary theory says that just as you and your cousin share a grandmother,

humans and apes—and, if we go way back, all other species—originally emerged from the same organism. This was a controversial idea at the time, and many contemporary caricatures depicted Darwin himself as an ape. Despite the backlash, however, Darwin launched an irreversible process, and his theory of evolution gained ground. Eventually, more and more people came to believe that human beings have not always looked the way we do today, and that, just like other animals, we descended from earlier creatures.

Most people understand this concept at the level of anatomy—human beings and cave dwellers evolved from the same ancestors, and the physical traits that

made the cave dwellers better able to ward off predators, live healthier lives, and adapt to their environment survived and now live on in human bloodlines. But many people don't consider that Darwin's theories can also be applied quite readily to psychology. In fact, the same human characteristics that we tend to think of as differentiating us from other animals—the ways we think, feel, behave, and react—all began as evolutionary adaptations, and they've been bred into us over thousands of years. Just as we no longer have tails, Darwin thought, we no longer think in ways that were already not working to our advantage thousands and thousands of years ago.

The longer Darwin observed animals, the more he noticed connections between human and animal emotions and behavior. As a result, he began to view the difference between humans and other animals as one of degree, not of kind. A later work by Darwin, *The Expression of the Emotions in Man and Animals,* includes remarkable illustrations of this idea, not only in words but also in drawings by various artists and in early photographs. For example, chimpanzees are seen to sulk and pout in ways that make them look similar to humans. When a cat faces a predator, the cat's face widens in fear, not unlike what happens when a human being is frightened. When a macaque receives a pleasant caress, its face shows unmistakable happiness.

Darwin also recognized that human emotions remain very similar across different cultures. He identified many emotions—love, joy, devotion, anxiety, despair, grief—that appear to have universal expressions, and he theorized that such expressions serve to communicate our inner feelings to other members of our species.

THEN WHAT?

Darwin's ideas changed the direction of psychological thought in several ways. Later theorists became more interested in individual differences among people, and in how those differences might result from genetic factors as well as from long histories of varied adaptations. (This interest also has a darker side, involving theories of racial superiority and inferiority.) Darwin's work also opened up lines of research into intelligence and personality. Ethological psychology—another branch of psychology borrowed closely from Darwin's theories—was most famously promulgated by Konrad Lorenz, who looked at animals in their natural environments and observed such genetically ingrained behaviors as imprinting. (There exists some rather amusing footage of geese obsessively following Lorenz. The geese clearly believe that Lorenz is their mother, since his image became imprinted on them early in their lives, thanks to a gosling's survival-oriented genetic predisposition to attach to the first animal it lay eyes on during a critical early period after birth.)

KEY EXPERIMENT Charles Darwin made a series of observations during a nearly five-year journey aboard the *HMS Beagle* to survey various parts of South America. That journey didn't constitute an experiment per se, but Darwin's observations served as a major catalyst for the development of his theories. (Ironically, the ship's captain, Robert FitzRoy, originally hoped the voyage would substantiate the book of Genesis and give scientific discoveries a more biblical slant, but that goal went extinct, so to speak, when Darwin began observing animals in the Galápagos Islands off the coast of Ecuador.) Darwin was struck by the vast number of species within a single genus, most particularly in the case of finches and the species of tortoise for which the islands were later named. Even more remarkable than the number of different species within a genus was the fact that each species appeared to have developed its own characteristics as a specific adaptation to its own environment (for example, different finch species had different types of beaks that gave them access to different local food sources). It was already understood that human animal breeders can select for various characteristics, as breeders do with dogs, for instance. But Darwin's observations in the Galápagos Islands led him to conclude that nature, too, could select for particular traits, and that the traits most likely to be targeted by the process of natural selection were those most likely to be linked to an animal's survival.

WHAT ABOUT ME?

Think of something that really, really scares you. What came to mind? Was it spiders? Heights? Snakes? Lightning? Rats? If you thought of what is most likely to kill you in this day and age, you probably thought of cars, pills, guns, or maybe electrical outlets. But chances are that you, like almost everyone else, continue to feel most threatened by things that in no way represent the greatest dangers you actually encounter on a daily basis. What accounts for the fact that few people are walking around with a fear of electrical outlets, even though the modern psyche retains its fear of things like heights, snakes, storms, spiders, and open water? The answer is that fear of such things was very rational for our cave-dwelling ancestors. Those fears helped keep them alive. And our ancestors' fears also kept humans alive as a species, since our ancestors had a biological interest in keeping their genes going.

Speaking of which, what are the traits that you look for in a mate? There's a lot of variation in this area, of course, since different cultures have different standards of beauty. In addition, not all of us, whether we're gay, straight, or in between, are interested in mating solely for the sake of reproduction. Nevertheless, the traits that most people find sexually attractive do seem to reflect the desire to maximize human offspring's chances of survival.

A woman looking for a longer-term mate may tend to be attracted to a provider type—someone whose stability, trustworthiness, and even financial resources hint at the ability to provide for offspring. A man seeking a mother for his offspring may tend to look for traits like a nurturing personality, warmth, and kindness. And when it comes to purely physical traits, the profile pictures on any online dating site will quickly confirm that height and strength are thought to be attractive in a man, and that a curvy, feminine figure is seen as attractive in a woman. Both sets of traits signal youth and fertility, and they

seem to have seeped into human sexual desire, whether someone is hoping to have a baby or simply score a hookup. Across cultures, people of both sexes also tend to seek out traits that signal a basic level of genetic fitness, such as symmetrical facial features and a complexion free of apparent illness or infection. Interesting research has also suggested that a heterosexual woman's assessment of a man's attractiveness may vary according to where she is in her menstrual cycle, and that she may seek out even more masculine and symmetrical features while she is ovulating.

In short, much of the behavior that seems to come to us most naturally has not always been inherently human behavior. Instead, it reflects human adaptations to the environment over time. Those adaptations motivated our ancestors, as they also motivate us, to keep our genetic lines going. What feels to us like acting naturally is behavior that evolved to help keep us safe and make us smarter, stronger, and healthier.

Paul Broca

BORN 1824, Sainte-Foy-la-Grande, Gironde, France

DIED 1880, Paris, France

Educated at the University of Paris and the Hôtel-Dieu de Paris

BIG IDEA

Paul Broca's impact on psychology was so significant that a section of the brain bears his name. **Broca's area**, in the frontal lobe, is the part of the dominant hemisphere responsible for producing speech. (Most people are right-handed, and so in most people it's the left hemisphere of the brain that is dominant, which means that Broca's area, for most people, is in the left hemisphere.)

Broca's association with this area of the brain began when, as a surgeon, he encountered a patient who had been hospitalized for two decades. The patient's listening comprehension was solid—he could understand whatever was said to him—but he could speak only a single syllable. Broca examined the patient's tongue, vocal cords, and voice box and quickly deduced that nothing was physically wrong with them. Shortly afterward, when the patient died, Broca conducted an autopsy and discovered a large lesion in part of the brain's left frontal lobe. Broca's biggest idea was solidified right then and there: Damage to this part of the brain has a unique and specific effect on the ability to produce spoken words, even though this damage to the brain doesn't affect the ability to understand words.

Earlier theorists had attempted to put forth the idea of **brain localization**—namely, the notion that specific parts of the brain can be linked to specific psychological functions. Perhaps because they were theorists more than scientists, this idea had not gained currency in the prevailing scientific views of the time. But Broca's discovery spurred him to further study—he analyzed the brains of a dozen more deceased patients and noticed similar lesions. He was finally able to back up the idea of brain localization with concrete, systematic, empirical evidence that gave this idea research momentum.

Broca's original patient was suffering from what we now call **aphasia**, a term that refers broadly to a deficit in speech. The particular type of aphasia from which this patient suffered is called *expressive aphasia*, or now even *Broca's aphasia*. For this patient, language function as a whole was not lost—recall his ability to understand what was said to him—but his ability to speak was greatly compromised by the lesion in his frontal lobe. In the decade after Broca's discovery, a nearby area of the brain that accounts for language comprehension was identified and named for Carl Wernicke, a German neurologist. People who suffer from aphasia involving that area are able to talk fluently, but their utterances aren't put together in meaningful ways, nor can they understand what is being said to them. Their condition is called *receptive aphasia* or now, often, *Wernicke's aphasia*.

The discovery of such a clear correlation between the biological structure of the brain and particular kinds of abilities and behavior was momentous. It also confirmed that the brain is not a homogeneous structure but has different areas, each with its own characteristics. The latter discovery underlies much of brain research to this day.

THEN WHAT?

Broca's findings set the stage for long-term research into the brain correlates of various emotions and psychological functions, and for the broader study of the physiological determinants of behavioral traits. This area of research continues to the present and includes projects as sophisticated as the mapping of the human genome. Broca's findings also encouraged a key underlying element of physical anthropology—study of the implications of physical measurements of the brain.

WHAT ABOUT ME?

Broca's discoveries, and brain localization more generally, are sometimes associated more with bad news than with good. Consider a brain tumor, to take a stark example. A brain tumor's signs and symptoms can include an almost unlimited array of disruptions—memory loss, taste hallucinations, loss of balance, changes in vision, vomiting, muscular weakness—that affect sensations, behavior, emotions, and the personality as a whole. The fact that there is no single standard symptomatology for

brain tumors can sometimes be problematic from the standpoint of early diagnosis, since a person can easily brush aside the symptoms of a brain tumor. (It's also true that someone can be convinced of having a brain tumor when there's nothing wrong with the brain at all.)

Brain injuries, too, can have immediate and distinct consequences—trauma to the head can cause symptoms that vary widely according to which part of the brain has borne the brunt of the impact. In this respect, the most famous case, involving a railroad construction worker named Phineas Gage, predated Broca's discovery by 13 years. In 1848, Gage suffered a horrifying injury on the job when an iron rod penetrated his left cheek, pierced his skull, and emerged from the crown of his head. Gage survived and even recovered from the injury, but his personality was forever altered. The personality changes were not unexpected, of course, but they appeared to go beyond the emotional trauma of the injury. Before the accident, Gage was productive and organized, but now he became unpredictable and incapable of initiating plans or following through on them. Once mild-mannered, he now cursed up a storm. He became impatient, stubborn, and unable to work with others. The damage sustained by his brain changed his personality completely.

Even more fascinating are cases of foreign accent syndrome, which can appear after a brain injury or even after a severe migraine headache. The person affected by this syndrome starts speaking in unusual ways, and his or her previous pitch and cadence are significantly changed. This is not to say that someone with this syndrome necessarily speaks with the precise accent associated with specific foreign speakers, but rather that there is a striking alteration in voice mechanics. Research points to damage within the cerebellum, the part of the brain that controls motor movement, and to a misalignment between the jaw and the tongue so that words are uttered in a way entirely different from the person's previous speech patterns.

William James

○──●

BORN 1842, New York City, New York

DIED 1910, Tamworth,
New Hampshire

Educated at Harvard University

BIG IDEA

William James's *Principles of Psychology*, years in the writing, is a 1,300-page block-buster of a book, a panoramic journey through all aspects of psychology. In 1890, when it was published, it made such an authoritative splash that it was sometimes just referred to as the *James* (a later, briefer version came to be called the *Jimmy*).

William James had so many big ideas, and his impact on the field of psychology has been so vast and enduring, that it's hard to summarize the ways in which he was most influential. What we'll do here is consolidate his most noteworthy theories into three domains: his thoughts about habits, his theory of consciousness, and his beliefs about the nature of emotion.

In his writings about how habits develop, James came as close as he ever would to sounding like a behaviorist. He believed in free will, but he also hypothesized that a habit leaves an anatomical trace within the brain, creating a pathway that will become more and more entrenched as time goes by. This pathway serves, in effect, as a physiological way to keep someone in a rut and ever more likely to retain the habit. Nevertheless, James also saw habits as playing a role in preventing societal chaos, and as delivering a not-so-subtle kick in the rump to people who need motivation to do things that are sometimes difficult. These views are well in line with the school of functionalism, and indeed James is considered to have advanced that particular school.

The notion of the **stream of consciousness**, taken directly from *Principles of Psychology*, represents a departure from the structuralist view that thoughts can be individually and meaningfully broken down into their constituent elements. Rather, James saw thoughts as a constantly changing river, consistently without gaps and irreducible to its elemental components. He also wrote of consciousness as an individual matter—your thoughts are yours, and my thoughts are mine. James believed that consciousness could be selective (meaning that sometimes we pay attention to parts of things and sometimes we attend to wholes), and that it is purposeful. These ideas about consciousness, taken together, paint a picture much different from anything that had been theorized before. The notion of consciousness as running commentary (even in the literal sense, because we often speak our train of thought), invulnerable to easy division or categorization, is one that still has loyal adherents today.

William James also changed the direction of popular thought through the **James–Lange theory of emotion**, named for himself and the Danish physician Carl Georg Lange. This theory posits the exact opposite of the era's commonly held belief that emotion precedes physiological response; indeed, the James–Lange theory proposes that emotion is a response to the experience

of a physical sensation. For example, this theory says, when you see a rabid dog barreling toward you, it is not that first you feel scared, and that then you tremble and your heart races; rather, you see the dog, you tremble and your heart races, and only then do you feel scared. Since the time when it was first proposed, this theory has attracted significant challenges. Modern theorists accept it as partly explaining a possible relationship between physical sensation and emotion, but today other pieces of information are also seen as affecting emotional assessments of situations, and subjective emotional responses are understood as also sometimes causing physiological reactions.

THEN WHAT?

William James's influence was so far-reaching that he is often considered to have been the first true psychologist. Functionalism, cognitive psychology, and Gestalt psychology are directly rooted in James's theories, as is the pragmatist school of philosophical thought. The James–Lange theory of emotion, although it's accepted today only with modifications, underlies substantial modern research on the nature of physical arousal and its role in cognition and emotion.

WHAT ABOUT ME?

If you weren't in the habit of setting an alarm to get up in the morning for work, and if other people also didn't have that habit, then surely modern society would not run as smoothly as it does. We often think of habits in negative terms, but daily rituals like stopping at red lights and putting on clothes can be considered positive habits. And when we think of William James's relevance to modern life, we immediately think of his ideas about how to create new, positive habits.

James believed that in order to eliminate a negative habit (which he saw as a neural pathway, a literal rut in the brain) and chart a new course, it is necessary to start with as strong and decisive an initiative as possible. For example, if you want to cut out carbs, then start by clearing your pantry, and declare your intention loudly and clearly on Facebook. And you'd better heed James's beliefs about consistency, too—deviating from your new pattern too early can undo a ton of work. If you've ever strung together days of sobriety or seen your exercise routine completely undone by a vacation, then you know that one day's fall off the wagon can feel as if it's done more to destroy your new positive habit than the six months of practice you put in to establish it.

And though, as we've seen, the James–Lange theory of emotion is not without

its detractors, the possibility of its relevance persists. For example, have you ever drunk coffee that was particularly strong and then started to feel jittery, anxious, and worried? How long did it take you to realize that it was just the caffeine talking? To put this another way, your physical symptoms led you to believe that you must be on edge, but when you remembered having drunk that cup of strong coffee, you probably felt more comfortable. Deciding to smile, and then discovering that you actually feel happy; adopting powerful body language, and then feeling more confident; faking it till you make it—these are all positive examples of the James–Lange theory in action. As for negative examples, what better authority do we have than people who suffer panic attacks? It doesn't matter that the cause of a palpitating heart may be something completely undramatic, such as having eaten spicy food or walked briskly upstairs. The person whose heart is pounding interprets that sensation as threatening and frightening (we call this an *interoceptive* sensation). And when the physiological sensation starts, the negative emotions follow—a living, contemporary, very personal validation of the James–Lange theory.

Behavioral Psychology

Unlike biological psychologists, who believe that anatomy and physiology, along with ancestral history, can influence behavior, behaviorists believe that our experiences turn us into who we are, and that what we learn and observe of the outer world is almost enough to completely shape us. They focus on action and its quantifiable measurement. What stimuli did we notice yesterday, and how have those stimuli influenced our behavior today? What consequences, in terms of rewards and punishments, can most quickly teach us to choose to act certain ways in the future? Behaviorism at its most pure says that we are virtually a blank slate at birth, ready to be molded by our environments for better and for worse, and not fundamentally different from each other in terms of temperaments, subjective emotional experiences, or personalities. Behaviorists view the connections between our environmental influences and our life choices as being prime in their importance, superseding things like genetic predispositions or cognitive interpretations. Behaviorists often study animals and draw connections to humans, as they view the mechanisms of motivation for action as fundamentally similar across species. Early in the 20th century, the behaviorists singlehandedly shifted the focus of psychology from being concerned solely with the internal workings of the mind and emotions into a larger focus that included how we make our way, externally, through the world. That broadened focus remains today, and though behavioral psychology is now often combined with findings from cognitive psychology for a fuller picture, especially in terms of treatment for psychological challenges, the influence of its earliest theories remains strong and quite present in day-to-day life.

Ivan Pavlov

—●—

BORN 1849, Ryazan, Russian Empire

DIED 1946, Leningrad, Soviet Union

Educated at St. Petersburg University

BIG IDEA

Ivan Pavlov began his career as a researcher of the salivation response in dogs. His exploration of classical conditioning was a departure from past animal research, not only because of its focus on behavior but also because the dogs were studied for long periods of time without having to be killed for the sake of the experiments. Pavlov soon noticed the phenomenon of psychic secretions—drooling that happened even before food was in the dogs' mouths. When he began to explore repeated patterns of behavior, he started

calling this type of salivation a *conditional response* (the word *conditional*, in the original Russian, was translated as *conditioned* in English, and the term *conditioned response* has been used ever since).

To understand the fundamentals of Pavlov's conditioning theory, you need to know a few additional key terms. An **unconditioned stimulus** is a stimulus (such as meat powder) that will automatically evoke a response (such as salivation in dogs), naturally and without the need for any conditioning to have occurred. A **conditioned stimulus** is a stimulus (such as a musical tone) that may eventually evoke a response (such as salivation in dogs), but first it will need to be paired often enough with an unconditioned stimulus (such as meat powder).

In his work with dogs, Pavlov showed that, at first, a conditioned stimulus will not automatically evoke a response. For example, dogs have no reason to associate a musical tone with food, and so a musical tone, in theory, won't make dogs drool any more than a crayon would. But Pavlov's eureka moment came after he repeatedly paired a conditioned stimulus (a musical tone) with an unconditioned stimulus (meat powder), often enough that the musical tone eventually evoked the salivation response on its own. In other words, even though dogs have no reason to associate a musical tone with food, the tone can be associated with food often enough that it will cause dogs to salivate even when no food has been presented.

Another key component of Pavlov's theory is his finding that the more times a conditioned stimulus and an unconditioned stimulus are paired, the stronger the association becomes, and the stronger the response that the conditioned stimulus can trigger all on its own. Pavlov showed that repeated pairings are key and that there also has to be **temporal contiguity**—in other words, the presentation of the unconditioned stimulus (the meat powder) has to closely *follow* the presentation of the conditioned stimulus (the musical tone). If they're presented at the same time, or in reverse order, the attempt at conditioning will fail.

Pavlov believed that **trace conditioning** can occasionally occur if the experience of the conditioned stimulus has already faded before the unconditioned stimulus is presented. He also observed the complete extinction of the response (salivation in dogs) after the conditioned stimulus (the meat powder) had been presented enough times on its own, without the presentation of the unconditioned stimulus (the musical tone), so that the dogs gradually learned that the musical tone was no longer going to bring them food, and their salivary glands eventually stopped reacting to the musical tone. (Nevertheless, Pavlov showed that spontaneous recovery of the association between the conditioned stimulus and the unconditioned stimulus can sometimes take place.)

Pavlov also discovered that the conditioned stimulus need not be presented in exactly the same way each time in order to evoke the conditioned response. Its presentation just has to be similar enough each time. He attributed this phenomenon to what he called **stimulus generalization**. In other words, the tone doesn't always have to be exactly the same pitch. Pavlov also taught the dogs what he called *discrimination*, or the ability to differentiate between gradations of the same stimulus; in this case, the dogs learned that a high-pitched sound from a tuning fork would bring food, and a lower-pitched sound would not. But Pavlov noticed that if he forced the dogs to discriminate too much, by using pitches that were too similar, they would exhibit what he referred to as **experimental neurosis** and become quite anxious and discouraged.

Pavlov's holy grail was **higher-order conditioning**, or using a conditioned stimulus (such as a musical tone) as if it

were an unconditioned stimulus (such as meat powder) as the basis for an altogether new round of conditioning. He found, however, that with each level of higher-order conditioning, the response (salivation) lost some of its strength. He believed that second-order conditioning, just one level up from the original conditioning protocol, is attainable but that third-order conditioning is virtually impossible. Nevertheless, the idea of higher-order conditioning served as the foundation for the concept of behavioral chaining, whereby links are created between different layers of stimuli and responses.

Pavlov was not without his detractors. Since he was first and foremost a physiologist, some academics of his day felt that his conditioning experiments strayed too far from real science. Psychologists today, of course, beg to differ.

THEN WHAT?

Though Pavlov is not usually considered to be the true founder of behaviorism, you could certainly make the case that he should be given this distinction. His theories directly influenced John B. Watson, the originator of the term *behaviorism*, who took a keen interest in classical conditioning. Conditioning theories that came later (such as B. F. Skinner's operant, or instrumental, conditioning), and that involve reward-oriented behavior rather automatic behavior, also drew on Pavlov's original ideas. Pavlov emphasized the importance of the role of the environment over that of the mind when it comes to the reasons behind our actions, and behaviorism followed his lead for decades afterward.

WHAT ABOUT ME?

Any automatic physiological response in humans is subject to conditioning, which has effects that may be helpful or not so helpful. Sexual arousal, for instance, is often conditioned to occur in direct relation to stimuli that have been associated in the past with sexual arousal. Maybe a couple has a special word, song, or physical signal that serves to set the mood. A less pleasant conditioned response has to do with nausea. Perhaps you once got food poisoning after eating bad mussels, and now the very sight of mussels is enough to turn your stomach. There is even a connection between classical conditioning and the body's response to drugs and alcohol. Let's take alcohol tolerance. The term *tolerance* refers to the need to drink more and more just to get the same effects that a single drink used to provide. Tolerance is thought to occur in part because the body develops a physiological reaction that tries to counteract the effects of alcohol when drinking begins. The body learns to secrete alcohol antagonists, and it takes note of the characteristics of alcohol (notably its smell and its taste) in order to become adept at this process. When someone with a significant alcohol tolerance cracks open a beer, his or her body anticipates the likely effects and goes into action, just as it's been conditioned to do. The same physiological phenomenon is at work when someone uses heroin after a period of abstinence and then dies from an overdose, even though the amount used was not greater than before. In this case, the body, which has stopped automatically counteracting the substance, is caught off guard.

John B. Watson

BORN 1878, Travelers Rest,
South Carolina

DIED 1958, New York City, New York

Educated at Furman University and
the University of Chicago

BIG IDEA

John B. Watson had little use for either
structuralism or functionalism, as he
thought that both were too bogged
down in questions about the nature of
consciousness. Watson was not one for
studying introspection; he wanted to
study externally measurable behavior.
He rejected psychology's prior focus on
understanding the mind, and his 1913
article and address "Psychology as the
Behaviorist Views It" not only coined

the term *behaviorism* but also forever
changed the course of psychology.

Watson saw behavior as predictable,
controllable, and always the result of
conditioning. He believed that there is no
such thing as instinct and that no aspect
of behavior is inborn. This stance came to
represent what is known as *radical behaviorism*, which, true to its name, says that
behavior, almost like a mathematical equation, is the direct and unambiguous product
of environmental forces. Watson endorsed
Pavlovian conditioning and extended it to
the areas of learning and emotion, believing
that temporal contiguity is important above
all else. In other words, he said, as long as a
conditioned stimulus and an unconditioned
stimulus are presented closely together
and in the proper order, learning will
occur. Watson also believed that there are
no meaningful differences between animals

KEY EXPERIMENT Watson's work on a baby named Little Albert is no doubt his most famous experiment, and not necessarily in a good way. Though it certainly illustrated his principles of conditioning quite well, it is hard not to cringe at the damage that it did to the child.

Little Albert, whose actual identity is still being debated more than 80 years later, was 11 months old and not overly emotionally reactive. At the start of the experiment, he was afraid only of loud noises. In the first part of the experiment, Albert was placed on a table, and a white rat was set in front of him. As soon as Albert touched the rat, a very loud clang was produced with a metal bar. Albert immediately fell forward and whimpered.

Once was all it took. When the rat was presented on its own a week later, Albert tried to crawl off the table so fast that someone almost didn't get there in time to catch him. Albert's fears were then shown to have generalized to hair, a rabbit, a dog, and even a Santa Claus mask.

A month later, Albert's fears persisted, though they had lessened a bit. Most egregiously, Watson didn't try to remove the conditioning; he simply never bothered to try to extinguish Little Albert's fears, and he appeared unconcerned about the possibility of lasting consequences, even though he acknowledged that such consequences were indeed possible. In fact, Watson criticized what he imagined would be the Freudian interpretation of Albert's fears 20 years later; to Watson, the experiment was simply all in a day's work of providing scientific proof for behaviorism and rejecting other doctrines, regardless of the consequences.

Watson did eventually advise his research assistant, Mary Cover Jones, on how to remove the fear conditioning they had created in a different boy, Peter. Thankfully, the conditioning could be removed through the process of breaking the association between the unconditioned stimulus and the conditioned stimulus, by way of extinction.

and humans when it comes to conditioning and learning. Unlike Pavlov, he brought humans into the lab so as to look at human conditioning directly, though Watson's earliest research involved learning in rats.

Watson also believed that psychology as a science should be studied empirically and quantitatively, and his behaviorist manifesto, basically redefining what the word *psychology* meant at the time, ushered in an almost exclusive, decades-long focus on behavior rather than on the nature of the mind.

It is not that Watson had no interest in emotion. On the contrary, his research on infants led to his belief that three specific emotions are inborn: fear, rage, and love. But he believed that these emotions can be triggered automatically only by a very small number of stimuli (loud noises for fear, or tickling and patting for love, for example). Watson hypothesized that conditioning is what expands these emotional responses to other situations. So a child is not innately destined to love his mother but does so because she caresses him the most. Future love relationships will simply be the results of conditioning and of associations formed with feelings of love. Thus, according to Watson, emotional responses have nothing to do with personality or genetics.

Watson thought the same thing about remembering things and using language. He saw both as conditioned responses that are not qualitatively different from other types of behavior. He'd say that we remember things because of associations with other things, associations that have become solidified in our minds. We learn to speak because we are prompted to do so by external triggers.

Watson was also instrumental in popularizing psychology for the masses and showing that its influence can have practical applications—most specifically, helping people make money. Dismissed from his post at Johns Hopkins University because

of a scandalous affair with his teaching assistant (they later married, after Watson left his wife), he went on to become an advertising executive in New York. He put his expertise to use by helping corporations persuade people to buy their products, and his theories gained currency in this decidedly nonacademic arena. Once again, in this new setting, Watson invoked the trio of fear, rage, and love. He believed that these three emotional responses, along with appeals to needs or habits, can motivate consumers to buy a product. His ad campaign for a baby powder used fear as a motivator and focused on the need for frequent use of the powder to prevent babies from getting sick. Watson was also an early adopter of celebrity testimonials (pair a celebrity with a product, and people will feel about the product the same way they do about the celebrity) and the use of demographic information to target different segments of the market (not unexpectedly, given his focus on metrics and measurable behavior).

Unfortunately, Watson's strict, black-and-white beliefs about the nature of behavior also extended to the idea that children should not be given much affection. He felt that it is all too easy to spoil children with overt displays of love, and that parents who do so will raise children who are not able to cope with the world. Watson believed that parents should treat children as young adults, never hugging or kissing them but instead shaking hands. He had an abject hatred of mawkish, sentimental dealings with kids and felt

that such displays should be avoided at all costs. It is worth noting that his two sons condemned his approach, and, sadly, one died by suicide years later.

THEN WHAT?

By ushering in the era of behaviorism, Watson laid the groundwork for subsequent researchers, such as B. F. Skinner, who would expand its reach and applications. Watson set the stage for environmental influences to be viewed as worthy of study, and his crossover from academia to advertising opened up a world of market-research techniques. Some of behaviorism's best applications in clinical settings have to do with diminishing phobias and fears through techniques like systematic desensitization, which remains relevant to this day.

WHAT ABOUT ME?

Has a particular smell ever reminded you of a certain time in your life or even brought back the emotions you felt at that time? Maybe it was the fragrance of a perfume or the aroma of a food, or maybe the pungent smell of burning wood reminded you of the potbellied stove your grandparents had, and of the love you felt for them. Your responses were neither inborn nor automatic to those particular stimuli.

Instead, over time, you experienced those stimuli often enough in association with particular emotional states—love, comfort, excitement—that later on, even years later, those stimuli could evoke those emotional states on their own. For the same reason, music can pack quite an emotional punch. We may very well have some biological affinity for music itself, but many of the hooks and riffs and melodies that most stir us probably do so because of the emotional conditioning that was taking place while we listened to those songs over time.

Watson, of course, believed that not just pleasant emotions but also, most notably, fear can play a fundamental role in everyday conditioning. Have you ever felt creeped out by something and not been sure why? For example, your fear of a dilapidated, windowless van in a deserted parking garage is not instinctual but stems from the fact that this stimulus has been associated with enough horror movies or warnings from your parents that it has become almost certain to evoke a conditioned response of fear in you.

Since John B. Watson's time on Madison Avenue, advertisers have become much more sophisticated in their ability to make claims that, for all their flamboyance and extravagance, are never quite overt or explicit. TV commercials suggest that if you use certain products, you will be more sexually attractive, more socially beloved, or more financially successful. Of course, the advertisers aren't technically making those promises, but their hope is that as the products are repeatedly paired with those associations, you will also associate the products with them and eventually be motivated to put your money where your deepest insecurities are.

Edward Thorndike

○━━━●

BORN 1874, Williamsburg, Massachusetts

DIED 1949, Montrose, New York

Educated at Wesleyan University, Harvard University, and Columbia University

BIG IDEA

Edward Thorndike's **law of effect** was his biggest idea. It is behaviorism in a nutshell. It states that a behavior that evokes a pleasurable response is more likely to be repeated than a behavior that evokes an unpleasant one. This became a fundamental tenet of later conditioning theories. Thorndike eventually refined this idea even further, saying that rewards work much more effectively to strengthen learned responses than punishments do to deter undesired responses.

Thorndike also put forth the **law of use** and the **law of disuse**. The former says that the more frequently a stimulus and a response are connected, the more ingrained the resulting association will become. And the latter is its counterpart— the longer a stimulus and a response have been disconnected, the less ingrained the connection will become. Thorndike built on Pavlov's theories of classical conditioning by delving further into the concept of learning; in fact, we can consider him the first educational psychologist. Like the behaviorist pioneers before him, Thorndike was an empiricist, interested above all in measuring and quantifying his findings.

Thorndike called his overarching theory **connectionism**. This term refers to the application of conditioning

principles to learning; the name came from the idea that learning is always the result of the connection between a stimulus and a response. Thorndike also did work that altered the way reading and spelling were taught. He analyzed the frequency of words found in various children's works, and from them he compiled dictionaries specifically for children. His rationale was that language learning would be improved through greater focus on common words than on less common ones. That no one before Thorndike had tried such a rational, practical approach may seem surprising in retrospect, but it took Thorndike's interest in the intersection of data and education to bring that change about.

Thorndike created scales to assess students' growth across various areas, from arithmetic to handwriting, and these led to his development of several intelligence tests. And he advanced the idea that intelligence has different aspects—that a person can be strong in one area but not in another, or that someone can understand advanced calculus but not have the spatial wherewithal to figure out which way to turn in order to get back on the freeway.

KEY EXPERIMENT Edward Thorndike used animal research to formulate many of his additional theories on learning, and his version of the puzzle box was instrumental in many of his findings. It had wooden slats that the animals inside could see out of, and it was rigged to offer a particular way of escape—often a foot pedal, as we saw in his work with cats. (In a departure from other puzzle boxes that had been developed, this means of escape was inside the box itself, and so it could be used to test a variety of animals, not just monkeys, which could use their hands to reach outside the box; in fact, Thorndike made various alterations to the box so he could test chickens, dogs, and even fish.)

In a typical experiment, a cat, annoyed at being trapped in the box, would at first sulk around and make its unhappiness known, in that unmistakable though not particularly endearing way that cats have. This reaction was particularly exacerbated when food was placed outside the box, in the cat's direct view. At some point, the cat would press the foot pedal by accident, an action that led to the happy surprise of the door's springing open. Of course, the cats got faster and faster with subsequent practice, though eventually they reached a maximum speed. They couldn't get better indefinitely, and their performance would finally plateau. Even if overall speed differed from animal to animal, the pattern of how they improved was similar. As we know, Thorndike referred to the plotted pattern of this improved performance as a learning curve, and he showed its relevance to a variety of different animals, including humans.

Also credited to Thorndike's research is the concept of **trial and error**, which he developed by studying cats and their process of learning how to escape from an enclosure, called a **puzzle box**, by pressing a foot pedal. As the cats tried to escape, they made errors, but they made fewer and fewer errors as the experiment went on. Thorndike's key finding was that multiple trials and multiple errors are necessary components of the learning process.

Tasks in which participants exhibit the pattern of a **learning curve** are those in which participants display gradual growth and decreased mistakes, but mistakes are not eliminated all at once. If sudden insight were to eliminate all errors, then the typical learning curve would show a steep spike in competence, but in fact the typical learning curve shows sloping upward progress. This is why, in our modern-day use of the phrase *learning* *curve*, we are getting it 100 percent wrong. A steep learning curve, which many people associate with something that will be hard at first to learn, actually indicates quick and easy improvement in performance. It's important to remember that the curve represents improvement in performance, not the difficulty of the task.

THEN WHAT?

Thorndike's work created the foundation for the study of learning and for the field of educational psychology as a whole. His theories also led directly to further developments within conditioning theory and were a direct influence on B. F. Skinner, whose theories of operant conditioning were an outgrowth of connectionism.

WHAT ABOUT ME?

Have you ever looked at your child's report card and wondered just what methods were used to quantify her learning? Though controversy over standardized testing has come to a fever pitch, Thorndike's idea that learning can be assessed and measured, just like any other behavior, and that different teaching techniques can be pitted against each other, to determine which one will lead to better outcomes, was a revolutionary notion that still underlies education standards today. And, when you really think about it, isn't it a relief that there are at least some specific standards by which your child can be assessed? If your child's teacher weren't

able to point to concrete, quantifiable metrics for math tests or book reports as the justification for an A, a B, a C, or a D, then what would the grade really mean? At best, it might not have much value; at worst, it might be biased.

Perhaps you take it for granted that practice makes perfect, but have you ever really thought about the mechanics of just why that's the case? It's because of trial and error, not mere repetition; the difference between the two is something Thorndike discovered and emphasized in his theories. Let's say you're trying to master a complex piano piece. You know that you'll get better the more you play it, but the reason is that with each trial, you are making errors—some big, some small—and with each of those mistakes, you take in information about exactly how you made the miscalculation and what you need to do to improve.

Let's think further about how you learn. Perhaps you've turned to the Internet to master a particular skill—making a hundred origami swans for your sister's wedding, installing your own garbage disposal, or making a perfect omelet. You may turn to YouTube, which has revolutionized the world of how-to instruction with millions of step-by-step videos. But what is the most helpful way to use the video—to watch it through once, close your laptop, and then go on your merry way, or to keep the video alongside you as you learn, stopping and starting as you try to master the task on your own? You may have noticed that you fare much better the second way, even if you thought you had it after watching the first time. Why? Any child can tell you: We learn by doing, not just by watching. You will learn to perform a certain procedure or behavior much better if you can actually participate in the process and can keep refining your technique through trial and error rather than just watching someone else do it, which keeps you from going through the learning curve yourself.

Thorndike's notion of connectionism also underlies motivation for learning. Recall his theory that the connection between the stimulus and the response must remain strong, and that a behavior that creates a pleasurable response is more likely to be repeated than a behavior that creates an unpleasant response. Now think of trying to help your child learn multiplication tables. When she finally gets an answer right, do you clap and praise and give a high five? Or do you say, "Okay—finally"? That would be the way to create a negative consequence for learning, whereas connectionism would tell us that with praise, the right answers will start to come much more frequently. Anyone who's learned that a preschooler responds much better to praise for doing what's right than to scolding for not having completed the same task sooner has seen Thorndike's theories in action.

B. F. Skinner

BORN 1904, Susquehanna,
Pennsylvania

DIED 1990, Cambridge,
Massachusetts

Educated at Hamilton College and
Harvard University

BIG IDEA

Further pushing the "radical" in radical
behaviorism was B. F. Skinner. He believed
that nothing about an organism's individual physiology could explain behavior; our
actions are solely responses to environmental stimuli. To Skinner, genetics are
important only in the sense that they pre-
program us to be able to learn behaviors.

Skinner made the leap between Ivan
Pavlov's classical conditioning and what

he himself called *operant conditioning*;
according to Skinner, Pavlov's conditioning prepares a dog for food, but his
own conditioning actually spurs the dog
to get the food. Using his own version of
a puzzle box, which came to be known
as the *Skinner box*, he refined and standardized experimental protocols and
showed the world that lever-pressing
behavior is just as tangible and measurable as the salivation reflex. Thus
a new round of research was born.

Skinner used the term *operant conditioning* because it refers to behaviors
that operate on the environment in order
to produce consequences. He argued that
it is those consequences that determine
whether the behavior will ever be exhib-
ited again. Of course, this idea is similar
to Edward Thorndike's connectionism.

But Skinner's most groundbreaking contributions were what he called **schedules of reinforcement** and the proof of their crucial role in determining the strength of conditioning. He discovered that the patterns of the pairings between responses and rewards can greatly affect how strong the connections are. So you can train an animal to press a lever for food even if food is not presented every single time the lever is pressed. In fact, there are certain schedules of food presentation that will make the animal more likely to press the lever and to keep doing so.

Skinner, along with the behavioral psychologist Charles Ferster, proposed three main categories of reinforcement schedules:

» *Continuous reinforcement* is optimal for beginning to establish an association between a behavior and a reward. In this situation, every time a behavior is performed, a reinforcer, or motivating reward, is given.
» An *interval schedule* of reinforcement has the reinforcer being given after a certain amount of time, no matter how many times the behavior has been performed.
» A *ratio schedule* requires the behavior to be repeated a certain number of times, no matter how long it takes, before the reinforcer is given.

There are also two more delineators of reinforcement schedules:

» A *fixed* schedule of reinforcement is one in which the reinforcer is given methodically and predictably.
» A *variable* schedule of reinforcement will, as its name implies, vary over time and is not as predictable.

When you work for a salary and your paycheck comes every two weeks, whether you've taken a day off or not, that schedule of reinforcement is a fixed **interval schedule.** It's a fixed amount of time that brings the paycheck. But let's say instead that your job pays you a certain bonus after every third sale you make, with no base salary at all. That is a fixed **ratio schedule** because you get paid only when you exhibit the behavior of making a sale three times. As a wage earner, you would find a variable interval schedule of reinforcement much more frustrating. Your paycheck would come after a particular period of time, but that time period could vary widely and unpredictably from one paycheck to the next. A variable ratio schedule would also be disheartening because you would get bonuses after a certain number of times you performed certain behaviors at work, but the number of work behaviors needed in order for you to be paid would vary from bonus to bonus.

Skinner found that, on the whole, ratio schedules induce behavior at higher rates because they facilitate connections between behavior and reinforcers. You see fairly quickly and clearly how performing a certain action causes the reinforcer to

be given. And variable schedules tend to create behavior that is harder to extinguish, or get rid of. That's because, in those situations, you never know exactly when the reward might be right around the corner, so you may think: *Why quit now?*

This is a good time to point out that the term *negative reinforcement* does not mean what most people think it means; it actually refers to the removal of a stimulus rather than to an unpleasant consequence. So while many people think of positive reinforcement as a reward and negative reinforcement as a punishment, this isn't really the case. In

conditioning models, the balance of "positive" versus "negative" simply involves the presence or absence of a stimulus. Punishment, of course, involves situations that will make a behavior less likely to be repeated, whereas reinforcement makes a behavior more likely to be repeated. Both punishment and reinforcement can be positive and negative according to whether a stimulus is present or absent.

Skinner also showed that **shaping** can happen: If you reinforce someone's attempts that are in the ballpark of a desired behavior and try to guide those attempts accordingly, you can get them closer and closer to the response you want. Perhaps most famously, Skinner showed this with piano-playing cats, Ping-Pong-playing birds, and vacuum-cleaning pigs. He even partnered with the US military to train pigeons to guide missiles and saw some success, though funding for that project eventually lapsed.

Later in his career, Skinner combined his behaviorist principles with utopian ideas, writing the novel *Walden Two*, a reference to *Walden*, Henry David Thoreau's treatise on living in natural and simplified surroundings and relying solely on oneself. In Skinner's novelistic version of utopia, a group of people forms a community where each person can engage in work, hobbies, and the arts. The behaviorist catch, of course, is that no one in the community is thought to have free will or really much true freedom at all, as the community's members act in accordance with what the communal environment reinforces within them. Though the title of Skinner's additional book on the same theme, *Beyond Freedom and Dignity*, certainly sounds anything but utopian, its premise is that we should all attempt, as much as possible, to maximize the societal benefits of our behaviors.

Finally, Skinner argued that language is not qualitatively different from any other behavior; it is learned through repetition and reinforcement, just like anything else. This came to be another aspect of radical behaviorism, eventually bringing great controversy and dissent.

THEN WHAT?

Skinner consolidated and revolutionized behaviorism into a force that shaped mid-20th-century thought. His reinforcement schedules and operant conditioning models have influenced the development of psychological treatments for disorders as varied as obsessive-compulsive disorder and substance abuse. Skinner's behaviorist views went head to head with the nativist views of Noam Chomsky in a highly publicized debate where the two men presented opposing theories of language development.

WHAT ABOUT ME?

Skinner's schedules of reinforcement can be seen to underlie our behavior and motivation, in everything from work life to child discipline to gambling.

Let's start with a slot machine. You probably know that, overall, you against this one-armed bandit is statistically a losing proposition—casinos aren't so shiny and huge for nothing. And yet many of us may continue to put our money into a slot machine, over and over again, even when we lose every time. Why is this?

The answer is Skinner's variable reinforcement schedule. The hardest schedule on which to extinguish a behavior, it is the reason that you are still tempted with each trip to Vegas, and it's the cause of the difficulty you have in finally knowing when to fold 'em. You know that a slot machine pays sometimes, and sometimes it pays quite big. And whether a slot machine will pay is determined not by what time it is, but by how many times it's been spun. Oh, how difficult it can be to walk away when you know that just one more spin could send the whole thing exploding with bells, lights, whistles, and a big wad of cash!

Variable reinforcement schedules are also part of why so many of us are so addicted to our smartphones. After all, if you keep scrolling, checking, and refreshing enough, you will sometimes find something quite interesting. Perhaps you've had the unsettling realization that you grab your phone almost automatically, feeling somewhat uneasy without it. This is because you feel the need to engage in the behavior of checking for updates or, at the very least, listening for the "ding" that indicates them. It's the variable ratio schedule—some amount of checking your phone will pay off, but you're never sure what that amount will be. You know that the "ding" could just be spam from a restaurant whose mailing list you signed up for in order to get a free appetizer. But it also could be news from an old friend, a "job well done" acknowledgment from your boss, or a funny story from your sister. And so you continue, with your behavior proving particularly hard to extinguish.

Let's think about the motivation to work. Have you ever started a blog, only to have it gradually peter out after a few months, despite your best intentions? You may have cursed yourself for being so undisciplined; after all, you enjoy blogging more than going to your job, and perhaps you even had hopes of eventually developing an empire that would allow you to quit work altogether and be supported as a full-time blogger. And yet you just couldn't seem to stick to a schedule. That is likely because writing a blog post was not paired with any tangible reinforcement. You love the overall blogging concept, and you know it will take time to build an audience, but there are no consequences for any individual post, and there's no direct reinforcer for writing one. You don't have a schedule of reinforcement at all except for the vague good feeling you get from writing. But when only your Aunt Edna appears to have read your posts, that's not quite enough to keep you going. Your day job, on the other hand, gives you a paycheck every two weeks without fail, and if you were to suddenly stop showing up for that, the paycheck would eventually become a no-show as well. So the behavior of your going to work will likely continue to be much more reliable than the behavior of your writing posts for your blog.

Childrearing is, for many, the hot spot of behavioral reinforcement. Never does it seem more crucial to create motivation for specific behaviors than when you're trying to convince a tiny human to get up off the floor at Target and stop screaming. A time-out is a classic negative punishment—again, not because it actively presents an unpleasant stimulus per se, but because it takes away the positive stimulus. There is the absence of reward:

no playing, no parental attention, and no ability to move around and be stimulated during the allotted period of the time-out. For many kids, of course, there is certainly the presence of unpleasant stimuli—the tear-inducing sound of their siblings having fun when they are not. But you put the child in a time-out because you are hoping to extinguish the behavior you saw and don't want to see recur, and because you want to break whatever association it has with any kind of reward.

Sticker charts, clicker training for dogs, and token economies are all inherently Skinnerian concepts. In fact, we have come to think of them as such fundamental tools for motivation that we may no longer even think about the psychological mechanics that underlie them, or about the exact connections that we are trying to create between our behaviors and the ways they are reinforced.

Psychotherapy

When you think of the word *psychologist*, there's a good chance that it's not a researcher in a lab coat whom you visualize first. It's likely a friendly looking man or woman sitting in a comfy chair and motioning for you to do the same, looking at you expectantly and offering to listen to what is troubling you. Ultimately, the goal of psychology and psychologists is to help people. And even psychological research should always have this question in mind: How do its results apply to humans in the real world, and how can those results help treat emotional pain and inspire people to live the fullest, healthiest lives possible?

It's been the pioneers of psychotherapy who have most pushed this goal forward. Psychotherapists are, by definition, practitioners in the field, putting theory into action and directly interacting with people to help them understand themselves. Through theory, research, and practice, they have developed interventions and techniques to help treat emotional distress and develop healthier, more functional ways of interacting with others and with the world as a whole. They help challenge unhelpful or dysfunctional thoughts and can be part devil's advocate, part philosopher, part cheerleader, and, above all, good listeners and interpreters.

Psychotherapists are blessed with the privilege—which is also a great responsibility—of being let in on another person's deepest emotional workings. They are in a room with individual people who are troubled, sometimes greatly. And they are charged with the task of proving that all the psychological research actually matters. Can they make a difference, human to human? The following psychotherapists did, and they changed the field in the process.

Sigmund Freud

BORN 1856, Moravia, Austrian Empire

DIED 1939, London, England

Educated at the University of Vienna

BIG IDEA

There is no name in modern culture more closely associated with the field of psychology than Sigmund Freud's. It's not just that a **Freudian slip** makes for a convenient and inexpensive Halloween costume—though it does—but that his theories of the mind have been absorbed indelibly into our language, our cultural beliefs, and our understanding of who we are as people. Freud wrote extensively, often beautifully, about the psychological forces behind our actions. And while some of his theories are downright cringeworthy, and many suffer from the lack of systematic empirical scrutiny, he nonetheless had several ideas about human nature that were right on target and that revolutionized the way our culture thinks about the human psyche. And these ideas helped push forth psychology to be studied in ways that it never had been before.

Freud's biggest overarching contribution to psychology was his passionate argument that the **unconscious mind** plays a very meaningful role in our behavior. By *unconscious* he meant thoughts and feelings operating beneath the threshold of ordinary awareness. In *The Psychopathology of Everyday Life* (1901), Freud gave detailed evidence for the unconscious mind: his observations of "slips of the tongue," as he called them, or even "slips of the pen." In these cases, people accidentally substituted a different word for the one they had intended to say, but the word that came out instead was much more revealing—sometimes embarrassingly so—of their real feelings.

Freud would say that we can sometimes sense our unconscious mind's presence, as when something is right on the tip of our tongue. We can't come up with the word we want, but we know it exists right beyond our awareness. In those moments, what is it that we're aware of? Freud would say that it's the ever-present unconscious, always looming just below our immediate awareness. Some things we may attempt to push as far down as possible, repressing them in an attempt to keep from feeling pain or discomfort.

Freud's theories incorporated both the unconscious mind and the conscious mind. He believed that within the psyche are opposing forces called the **id** and the **superego**. The id is made up of the animalistic desires we are biologically prone to; Freud wholeheartedly believed that our inherent nature, in its most-stripped down state, is just as base as that of your average beast and includes things like lust, aggression, hunger, and thirst. The superego, on the other hand, is the internalization of all the values, rules, and expectations that we absorb from living in a particular society and culture and in a particular family: *Don't run with scissors! Don't punch your friend! Don't eat a seventh bowl of curds and whey!* Naturally, the id and the superego clash constantly. Imagine the proverbial devil on one shoulder, and an angel on the other, battling it out—and the poor entity left to constantly reconcile and referee these skirmishes is called the **ego**. Freud would say that the ego is essentially you and is housed within your conscious mind, unlike the superego and the id, which are submerged within the unconscious.

The angst and tension that result from these frequent battles don't make us feel very good. Anxiety rises with each conflict, and Freud said that this is where **defense mechanisms** come in. Defense mechanisms, Freud believed, are the thoughts and actions that we unconsciously trot out in order to soothe the conflict between the id and the superego. He listed many such mechanisms, from simple denial ("I'm not angry. Why would I possibly be angry, just because you forgot to pick me up at the airport? It's no big deal.") to projection, whereby we attribute our own feelings to someone else in order to believe that we're not feeling them ourselves (as when we shout at someone else to calm down). We see intellectualization: "Why was I driving by my ex-boyfriend's house at 3 A.M.? I didn't even notice that I did that. I simply had to go and fill my car up, and the gas station 16 miles from my house, but near his, has the best deals." And we see repression: "I have no memory of my dad hitting me at all. Apparently he did, and he was quite abusive, but I really don't know for sure that it ever happened."

Freud believed that our unconscious processes also seep into our dreams. Current theories say that during sleep our brains take out the neural trash, getting rid of the toxins and waste that have built up as by-products of our daily cognitive processes. And it's true that looking in someone's trash can sometimes tell you something meaningful about what's going on in his or her life.

Freud also had meaningful ideas on the nature of human development. He posited five **psychosexual stages** that we all go through and that unfold naturally as time goes by in our early lives. Though the stages themselves are no longer taken literally by most psychologists, the idea of qualitatively different developmental stages has stood the test of time. And Freud was right on target with his idea that something happening early in childhood can permanently affect development and continue to influence personality, emotions, and behavior in adulthood.

Freud's psychosexual stages have most certainly added color to our language. The first two, the *oral stage* and the *anal stage*, have become ingrained in our culture. The former is the stage from birth to about the age of two, when babies naturally want to put everything in their mouths as they sense their environment best that way and are always attuned to feeding. And the latter is the time when all focus shifts to toilet training. Freud's theory says that if something goes wrong during any of the stages, it will create a lasting disruption to mental well-being. Let's say a baby is either overfed or underfed. According to Freud, this disruption of the oral stage will lead to a later **fixation** that will

affect the person throughout the rest of his or her life. Similarly, an overly rigid or overly permissive approach to toilet training will create an anal fixation.

Some of Freud's ideas have been considered downright degrading, especially to women. He believed that women unconsciously suffer from penis envy, for instance. His theory of the **Oedipus complex**, named for the figure Greek myth, says that little boys secretly lust after their mothers and therefore want to kill their fathers in order to be able to possess their mothers sexually. Even though these theories are hardly progressive, it is nevertheless worth noting that Freud, unlike many others of his time, believed that homosexuality, though perhaps related to a disruption in early development, is "nothing to be ashamed of."

Finally, Freud's influence on therapeutic treatment represents one of his crowning achievements. He pioneered psychoanalysis, the first systematic psychotherapy of the modern era. It put a special emphasis on the patient-therapist relationship, with the concept of transference dictating that the patient would transfer some unconscious feelings onto the therapist, thus replaying other relationships from life outside the consulting room. This gave the psychotherapist an additional opportunity to help the patient heal. Though psychoanalysis has largely been overtaken by more modern, empirically validated techniques, such as cognitive behavioral therapy, it still has plenty of adherents, and there's

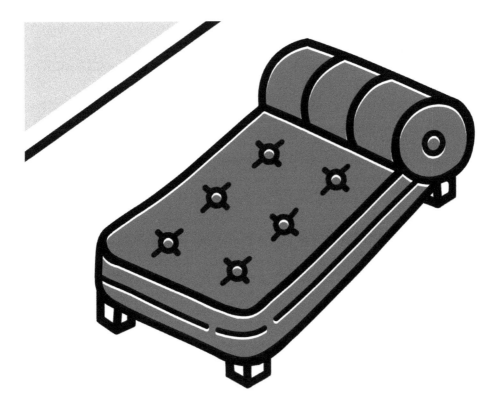

even an upswing in recent research. And its premise—that talking to an objective professional can help provide insight into the unconscious mind, healing distress and empowering one to live a healthier life—is the underpinning of modern talk therapy.

THEN WHAT?

Freud's ideas and his practice gave rise to psychoanalysis, which for many decades was the gold standard of psychological treatment, and which in turn has given rise to many different subtypes. His focus on the unconscious directly influenced several fields within psychology, with a newfound emphasis on the difference between what we are and are not aware of. Freud's theories directly influenced Carl Jung's ideas about the **collective unconscious**, Karen Horney's beliefs about **neurosis**, and Erik Erikson's theories of development.

WHAT ABOUT ME?

Do you have a recurring dream that appears only at specific times—when you are sick, when you feel particularly effective at work, when you are worried about a parent's health or are in a rut of arguing with your partner? The dream itself may seem incidental or even odd (you're back in high school, walking down a long hallway but unable to find your locker), but its continued presence at certain times in your life underscores its latent meaning. You are likely hashing out meaningful fears, hopes, or urges.

What about your friend who chews on everything, had a terrible time quitting smoking, and was a nail-biter through most of her childhood and teen years? Freud's followers would say this is a clear-cut case of an oral fixation. Freud himself would posit that perhaps her mother was overly strict about your friend's feeding schedule when she was an infant, and that your friend now exhibits the effects of a developmental hiccup that makes her continue to seek oral stimulation, a proxy for nourishment.

The term *anal* has gradually become shorthand for *anal-retentive*, the specific subtype of anal fixation that predisposes a person to obsessional inflexibility, perfectionism, orderliness, and neatness. Freud's interpretation would be that people are doomed to be overly rigid in this manner because of having suffered a disruption at the anal stage, perhaps because of always needing to hold back bowel movements during toilet training, and that they will always be anxious and have trouble letting go. (Personalities that are anal-expulsive, and who perhaps had virtually no order or structure regarding toilet training, are characterized by messiness and disorganization, and even by aggressive impulses and outbursts.)

Perhaps you know your own defense mechanisms pretty well—it's nearly guaranteed that your loved ones do. Do you tend to deal with emotional stress by keeping a stiff upper lip, not talking about your feelings, and pretending to everyone that you are fine? You may have a vested interest in denying your emotions and even repressing your stress because somewhere along the way your superego absorbed the idea, with your ego falling in line, that you just need to keep plowing forward without getting bogged down in your feelings. This could have happened via any number of messages that you grew up with: *Big girls (or boys) don't cry! Don't be a wuss! Get over it and move on!* But you may have noticed that your feelings don't automatically go away just because they've been buried. In fact, they may come back to haunt you in an emotional outburst or in a troubling dream.

Maybe you're much more likely to yell at your partner or your kids when you are stressed out about what's going on at work. Your loved ones did nothing except exist and happen to be in your vicinity on a day when you felt really angry at your boss. But one false move—something as inconsequential as a sock left on the floor—and you scream at them. Freud would call this defense mechanism *displacement*. Your superego has internalized the idea that screaming at your boss is not acceptable, but you have so much built-up distress that it has to come out somewhere. And so your ego dictates that you will displace all that fury onto a safer, more acceptable object—the spouse or children who cannot fire you.

Perhaps you've had the Freudian slip to end all Freudian slips, like the classic "Over there, on the bed—uh, the couch!" that slipped out of the actor Leonardo DiCaprio's mouth in the famous nude-portrait scene with Kate Winslet in *Titanic*. In that case, a sexually charged situation, the Freudian subtext was clear. Hollywood lore has it that the film's director, James Cameron, thought this was such a true-to-life slip that he left it in the film.

Carl Jung

BORN 1875, Thurgau, Switzerland

DIED 1961, Zurich, Switzerland

Educated at the University of Basel

BIG IDEA

Carl Jung (pronounced *Yoong*) is best known for taking some of Freud's ideas and giving them a softer, more positive, even spiritual spin, and for developing his own theories on the nature of personality. Jung was a unique figure in many ways, not the least of which was his simultaneous interest in mysticism and hard science. He did word-association studies that supported Freud's notion of repression and the unconscious, even as Freud's work was starting to lose a bit of credence in academic circles. But Jung's support was stalwart and meaningful, and Freud looked forward to the idea that Jung would take over the psychoanalytic movement, with Jung looking up to Freud as something of a father figure. Eventually their relationship frayed, however, and many attribute the break to their fundamental conflict over how much emphasis Freud put on infantile sexuality, and to Jung's new spin on the unconscious.

Jung broadened the notion of the unconscious, applying it in a more anthropological manner. His concept of the collective unconscious incorporates some of his mystical beliefs; he defined it as the psychological basis of everyone. To Jung, it was a universal concept, a treasure trove of our ancestors' hopes, urges, and fears that have been passed down to us. Jung would say we can see the collective unconscious reflected in the myths, folklore, and art that continuously reemerge across times and cultures. Religion has a place in this as well. Jung defined an **archetype** as a version of ourselves that lies within the collective unconscious, serving as the psychological counterpart to instinct, and directing our desires and behavior in ways that are outside our immediate awareness.

Jung defined the **persona** as the role that someone assumes in society—the outward manifestation of identity. The **shadow** is their unconscious, which may contain his or her animal nature. The **self**, for Jung, is the archetype that integrates everything, and its ultimate goal is to individuate itself and become fully realized.

Jung was much more interested in developing theories about mental energy than developing theories about sexual drives. He wanted to redefine the term *libido* away from the energies of the id—sex and survival urges—and toward the notion of what fulfills us mentally. As a result, Jung gave us the concepts of **introversion** and **extraversion**, which have to do with how we are driven, in the effort to feel most fulfilled and energized, either to seek out other people or to be alone.

Though the common misconception is that introverts are the nervous wallflowers at a party while extraverts are the ones laughing and shimmying on a table, the real definitions of the terms *introversion* and *extraversion* don't really correspond to the spectrum of shyness or social anxiety. Instead, Jung defined these terms as having to do with whether you are more oriented toward your internal world or toward the external world. Where do you get your energy? Does being around others revitalize you or drain you? If you had a day to spend however you wanted, would you fill it up with people or be on your own with your thoughts and a good book? Introverts relish the internal mechanisms of thoughts and ideas and are introspective and self-sufficient. Extraverts, on the other hand, need people around and are more externally focused. For most of us, extraversion or introversion is dominant, though in modern times a growing movement recognizes just how many of us are in the middle, or *ambiverts*.

Jung also identified four of what he called *psychological functions*: thinking, feeling, sensation, and intuition. We perceive the world through sensation and intuition, and then we use thinking and feeling in the decision-making process.

The theme of the relationship of opposites can be seen throughout Jung's work. The **anima** is what Jung calls the woman in the man, and the **animus** is the man in the woman. These ideas represent an opposing personality force, a piece within us that offers a dissenting view and helps shape us into who we are. Jung also introduced the Eastern artistic patterns of the mandala into Western culture, and he would even have his patients draw mandalas as an exercise in representing themselves. Jung felt that the mandala represents the whole self, and that it can bring forth opposing universal parts of the psyche and the collective unconscious. He found the

concept soothing—the tension relief of restoring order over chaos. He was drawn to the concept of a central part within a circle from which everything radiates, and which also connects all parts to the whole.

And, finally, **synchronicity** is a Jungian concept that has to do with the sometimes mysterious realm of coincidence. Jung believed that things are not random and that there is an order beyond the chaos. For Jung, moments that express synchronicity are the universe's way of giving us glimpses of everything being related. We can't see the causality behind the coincidence, but it is there, somewhere—a force outside our awareness.

THEN WHAT?

Jung's thinking has influenced not just psychology but also art theory, literature, and filmmaking. The **Myers-Briggs Type Indicator (MBTI)** is a personality test derived from Jung's ideas and is used to this day. Jung's ideas have found their way into certain psychotherapeutic schools of thought and are used by practitioners who call themselves Jungians, as well as by those in the broader field of depth psychology. Jung's focus on the importance of spiritual experience is even said to have influenced Bill Wilson, who cofounded Alcoholics Anonymous.

WHAT ABOUT ME?

You have quite possibly taken a variety of personality assessments on social media, from "What's Your Biggest Flaw?" to "Which *Game of Thrones* Character Are You?" But even more likely is that you have taken some variation of the MBTI, whether the legitimate version for a workplace organizational consultant or perhaps in the form of an oversimplified Facebook quiz. This is the assessment that gives you a four-letter personality type, one of 16 with names like ENFP or ISTJ. The MBTI was derived directly from Jung's ideas, and the letters indicating the 16 types correspond to his theories of extraversion versus introversion, intuiting versus sensing, feeling versus thinking, and perceiving versus judging. According to the MBTI's developers, someone's personality is defined by where it falls on each of these four spectrums. Intuiters rely on their "sixth sense," whereas sensers rely on more tangible stimuli; feelers are emotionally driven in their decision making, whereas thinkers like to look at pros and cons on a spreadsheet. It's rather amusing to imagine what Jung would say if he saw blazer-wearing consultants clicking open their briefcases and handing out computer-generated printouts derived from some of his major concepts.

The introversion/extraversion distinction may actually be worth a closer look within your own life. It's easy to assume that extraverts are socially confident and that introverts are shy and ill at ease around others. But this is not always the case. As mentioned, the extraversion/introversion dichotomy does not exactly correlate with social anxiety. There are introverts who are socially charming, very comfortable around others, and perhaps even born performers. But they are introverts because they need their space mentally—they easily tire of the company of others, and they live predominantly in their own heads. Similarly, there are plenty of shy extraverts—they very much want and need to be around others most of the time and often dislike being on their own, but they are somewhat nervous and anxious when actually interacting.

Perhaps you have noticed how certain stories are repeated across cultures. The universal themes of the hero, the scapegoat, the outsider, the wanderer, the devil, the fool, the trickster, the star-crossed lovers—from movie pitches to campfire stories, these archetypes are continually rehashed. You see them in stories big and small, for kids and for adults, and in cultures vastly different from one another. Might we all be related, across generations and oceans, deep within our most psychic cores? The tingle we feel when we visit ancient ruins or look at a centuries-old painting can make us suspect that Jung was onto something. Perhaps it's a glimmer of the collective unconscious—that it's not just our immediate life experiences but also our subjective emotional realities and deeper humanity that bind us to other people.

Karen Horney

•———•

BORN 1885, Schleswig-Holstein,
Prussia, German Empire

DIED 1952, New York City, New York

Educated at the University of
Freiburg, the University of Gottingen,
and the University of Berlin

BIG IDEA

Another member of the Commonly-
Mispronounced-Last-Name Club, along
with Carl Jung, is Karen Horney (that's
Hor-nigh), who bridged the seemingly
unbridgeable gap between Freudian theories and feminist psychology. Prior to her
big breakthrough, she focused on neurosis,
an area where her influence remains.

At its most basic, the term *neurosis*
refers to emotional distress, often in
the form of depression or agitation. In
modern-day thinking, it has become more
closely aligned with anxiety. Horney
viewed neurosis as a human condition, distinct from a person's one-time reaction to
a single stressful or traumatic encounter;
instead, she felt that neurosis follows us
everywhere and represents our attempts
to get by in day-to-day life. According
to Horney, some of us manage to do this
quite functionally, but others develop
fundamentally maladaptive traits as we
attempt to cope with the pressure of living.

Horney put forth the idea of **basic
anxiety**, which refers to a child's perception of being helpless and alone in a
scary and dangerous world. When a child's
relationship with his or her parents is
problematic, this anxiety spikes. Horney
theorized that parental inconsistency,
lack of warmth, or failure to consider a

child's emotional experience threaten the parent-child bond, and that the child then tries to minimize the resulting anxiety by developing defense mechanisms. Eventually, this pattern can make its way into the child's personality and lead to the development of more permanent traits.

This theory led to Horney's hypothesis of 10 **neurotic needs**, which she saw as so overwhelming and all-encompassing as to define a person. She classified the neurotic needs into three categories: those that compel us to comply (the need for affection, the need for a partner, and the need for simplifying life), those that lead us to withdraw (the need for independence and the need for perfection), and those that make us aggressive and turn us against other people (the need for power, the need to exploit, the need for prestige, and the need for personal achievement). These needs become neurotic only when they exist at dysfunctional levels or come into play too indiscriminately and too extremely in daily life. Most of us, Horney believed, can navigate these needs in healthy ways and reduce our interpersonal conflicts. And the more secure, tolerant, loving, and respectful our family life has been, the greater our chances of doing so. On the other hand, for a person who has developed neurotic needs, dysfunctional behavior can beget still more dysfunctional behavior and lead to the creation of vicious circles (or cycles). Moreover, Horney felt that healthy people see themselves as they are, while a neurotic person's identity is split into a despised

self and an ideal self. It's the gap between these two concepts of self that continues to perpetuate anxiety and neurosis.

Horney accepted several aspects of Freud's psychoanalytic theories, including the importance of the unconscious. But she disagreed with how much focus should be placed on biology and on sexual drives. She was more interested in the social roles and relationships that might underlie some of Freud's observations. For instance, she reworked Freud's theory of the Oedipus complex, removing its emphasis on sexuality and making it about a struggle for attention. Similarly, she discarded Freud's theory of penis envy, saying that any such feelings are less about the male organ itself than about the relative power and cultural acceptability of males as compared to females.

Horney was one of the first female psychiatrists, and her 1946 book *Are You Considering Psychoanalysis?* is considered by some to have been the first self-help book, and the first to have brought psychological interventions to those who were not in therapy.

THEN WHAT?

Horney's reworking of psychoanalytic theories to focus more on the relationship between parent and child was crucial for later explorations into attachment. This work led to giant leaps in the study of parent-child bonds, such as the explorations of John Bowlby and Mary Ainsworth (the latter became known for classifying

types of parent-child attachments in the "strange situation" task; see p. 121). Horney is often considered a neo-Freudian, a member of a school of thought that revised and adapted classic psychoanalytical constructs.

WHAT ABOUT ME?

Let's examine Horney's concept of neurotic needs further, through the need for social recognition or prestige. Everyone needs some validation and acknowledgment; it's a fundamental part of being human. But why and how does it become a neurotic need in certain people?

Let's say that as a child you really blended into the crowd—or, worse, that you stood out for the traits you didn't possess more than for those that you did possess. You didn't feel particularly good about who you were; you never seemed to have any qualities that people noticed in a positive way. Maybe you were an overweight kid in a classroom full of fit ones; maybe you were a struggling student in a home full of straight-A achievers. Or maybe your friends' parents knew interesting people, threw parties, and took trips, whereas you felt that you were missing out on a fuller life as your own parents chowed down on chips in front of the TV.

Perhaps you found ways to deal with your discomfort. Some kids immerse themselves in art, music, or sports, or they're saved by a couple of particularly good friendships. Or maybe you had an exceptionally solid and loving relationship with your parents, no matter how far outside the elite social scene they were. Perhaps you had a teacher who was particularly nurturing and helped you find your unique path in the world. If you had any of these things, you may have ultimately grown to feel recognized and valued for the person you are, not for who you are not.

But what if you didn't have any of these things? You grew more and more frustrated, and more and more defined by your perceived lack of social prestige. This preoccupation with what you lacked began to take over your personality, and you became obsessed with plotting ways to be popular in middle school. You worked two jobs in high school so as to have more money, and then you spent every dime on the latest fashions. You hung around only with people who were part of the in-crowd, pointedly ditching your next-door neighbor who had known you since

you were four. You even started acting out in ways that were just edgy enough to get you noticed and win you a seat at the cool kids' table. When you eventually got a job and were living your own life, you became a bona fide social climber, name-dropping left and right and trying to wrangle your way into the hottest clubs and the most exclusive parties. You couldn't stand not being in the know about a new product or trend, and your relationships remained rather superficial and shallow. Your social media accounts read like your unconscious: "Look at me! I am special and popular and exclusive!"

At this point, we're clearly looking at a neurotic need. It defines you and preoccupies you, getting in the way of your living your healthiest possible life on a day-to-day basis. It also represents what has probably become a hair-raising level of constant anxiety. Yes, most of us will get a jolt of pleasure from having a conversation with someone famous, or from getting to try a majorly hyped product before anyone else does. But only those with the neurotic need for social prestige will let the search for those jolts take over their lives.

Alfred Adler

BORN 1870, Rudolfsheim,
Austria-Hungary

DIED 1937, Aberdeen, Scotland

Educated at the University of Vienna

BIG IDEA

Alfred Adler's theories, which were
eventually combined into a school of
thought that came to be known as Adlerian
therapy, were almost too wide-ranging
for their own good. Adler is said to have
been incredibly generous with his insights
and not particularly concerned with
being given credit for the developments
he brought to the field, and so his influence is likely far greater than his name
recognition.

Many of Adler's ideas sprung from
psychoanalytic thought, and he was a
respected contemporary of Freud's. But
Adler gradually broke away from psychoanalysis and moved toward greater
emphasis on how we perceive ourselves
within our social relationships, in contrast to Freud's emphasis on biology
and on the instincts. Adler labeled his
approach *individual psychology* because
it emphasizes the individual as a whole
person rather than fracturing the self
into components, as psychoanalysis
has sometimes done. He also felt that
our thoughts about the future are more
worthy of focus than the events of the
past, and he didn't particularly believe
that past events predetermine anything
about who we eventually become.

Adler brought significant focus to
the notion of the *drive*—what motivates

us, and what we strive for. *Striving for perfection* is the term he used for the motivation to reach our goals and become our true selves. Sometimes this involves striving for superiority, which can be problematic in its emphasis on needing to be better than everyone else. Most famous is the counterpart to this, the concept of the **inferiority complex**. According to Adler, we all have some areas where we feel inferior, and we attempt to compensate for those deficits. Some of us do this in healthy ways, whereas others among us become overwhelmed by our inferiority. This may not even be a real inferiority but may instead be a perceived inferiority we've developed because of messages we've absorbed throughout our lives. When someone has an inferiority complex, it is maladaptive, and it takes over various aspects of functioning. The person will try constantly to overcompensate, to bridge the gap of his or her deficits. People with an inferiority complex are on a chronic quest to prove something to themselves and to others.

Adler's theories about our relationships with other people are best represented by his thoughts about **social interest**: our consideration of our communities and the people around us. How empathetic we are, how strong our relationships are, how well we interact with the people around us—Adler thought that these are all decent measures of how psychologically healthy we are in general. He felt that most psychological problems can be traced in large part to a lack of social interest—not to being introverted or shy, but rather to having no concern for our role with regard to other people, to caring only for ourselves, and to simply not giving a hoot about how we affect others.

Adler is also known as the first psychological theorist to have placed significant focus on birth order—the question of whether someone is an only child, the oldest, the youngest, and so on. He recognized that this information is more useful in general terms than as a specific formula for any given individual or family situation. But he noticed trends in personality that depend on one's role within a sibling group, with only children sometimes suffering from too much attention from their parents, oldest children tending more toward leadership and assertiveness, middle children sometimes struggling to find a place and perhaps even turning conflict-avoidant, and youngest children often being babied and prone to dream big but not to actually realize their potential. Once again, Adler acknowledged that in any given family, individual dynamics—and age ranges—might matter more, but his belief that sibling relationships can exert a powerful influence has stood the test of time as an insightful concept.

THEN WHAT?

Adler directly influenced a diverse range of theorists and practitioners. Elements of his work were later reflected in the humanistic therapeutic beliefs of Abraham

Maslow and Carl Rogers and in the existential approach of Viktor Frankl. Adler's more practical techniques of examining a patient's maladaptive behaviors can be seen as a forerunner of Albert Ellis's **rational-emotive behavior therapy (REBT)** and **cognitive therapy**, and Adler's spin on psychoanalysis, with its focus more on social relationships than on biological drives, influenced Karen Horney.

WHAT ABOUT ME?

Let's say I have a magic wand and can solve, overnight, a problem that you are dealing with, or that I can get you to a goal

you've been trying unsuccessfully to meet. You will wake up, and it will have been taken care of. What will your life look like then? That's not just a question—it's *the question*, as Adler named this therapeutic technique. He argued that there is a lot to be gained from having someone visualize what his or her life will be like after a problem has been solved or a goal has been met, especially because the person's ideal life, which he or she can clearly outline and seems to crave so wholeheartedly, may actually be exactly what the person is afraid of. In fact, he said, the very fact that the problem has been so long in the solving, or that the goal has been so long unmet, may reflect unconscious anxiety, which the person has been unable to face and overcome. Can't ever bring yourself to buckle down and finish that degree? Maybe deep down you're terrified of being done with school and facing the expectations and responsibilities of the "real world."

Of course, not every goal we set or fail to meet is associated with unconscious fears, and so this intervention isn't universally applicable. But its magic lies in the fact that it forces us to think of things from another perspective, and that it can lead us to acknowledge that sometimes the most persistent forms of self-sabotage come from secret fears we have not allowed ourselves to articulate. When we procrastinate on something that we supposedly want to do, or when we sit around wishing that a problem would just disappear, we may be fooling ourselves about exactly what's stopping us. Illuminating such obstacles can go a long way toward helping us realize our true potential.

Viktor Frankl

—●——●—

BORN 1905, Vienna,
Austria-Hungary

DIED 1997, Vienna, Austria

Educated at the University of Vienna

BIG IDEA

Victor Frankl had quite a life story. Not often do you see someone whose extreme experiences, part of a history that defined generations, have so clearly inspired his or her professional work and development.

In 1942, Frankl was a recently married doctor, living in Vienna, when he, his wife, his brother, and his parents were arrested and taken to the Theresienstadt concentration camp. Frankl had already spent a couple of years in quiet defiance of the Nazi regime; he had begun giving

patients false diagnoses to prevent them from being euthanized, per the Nazis' mandated policy toward the mentally ill (the Nazis' mentally sound targets were sent to concentration camps instead of being put to death). What happened next is tragic and all too familiar: All of Frankl's family members (except his sister, who had escaped Austria before the arrest of the others) died in concentration camps over the next few years. He learned this fact only upon his own liberation, in 1945. The horrors that he witnessed, and the pockets of hope that he occasionally experienced, helped inspire his most famous work, *Man's Search for Meaning* (originally published in 1946 in a German edition whose title was roughly "Nevertheless Saying Yes to Life").

Man's Search for Meaning has been a cultural touchstone for seven decades, and it continues to attract a vast audience. In the book, Frankl explores the horrors of his experiences in the concentration camp, his readjustment to life after his liberation, and his philosophy about states of mind. He consolidated these ideas into the foundation of a new type of therapy that he called **logotherapy**. Logotherapy involves the search for meaning, whereas Frankl felt that previous schools of psychotherapy had focused too much on the search for pleasure or the search for power.

In the most profoundly horrific of times in the concentration camp, Frankl was struck by the resonance of future-oriented thinking and by the lifeline that hope provided. He posited that being able to think of reuniting with loved ones or to dream of fulfilling some future goal is often the only thing that can keep a person's spirit from cracking. He asserted that to divide the world into good versus evil is misguided; those concepts overlap and exist everywhere, and he noted that he saw occasional kindness even in some of the guards at the concentration camp.

Sometimes, Frankl theorized, an **existential vacuum** is responsible for particularly unhealthy types of behavior. Things like boredom—the malaise we might feel during times of leisure, which he termed **Sunday neurosis**—can lead us to want to fill up those holes with material possessions, power, or superficial pleasures. But these don't provide relief, he argued, as they don't provide real meaning.

Meaning, Frankl posited, can emerge from three different types of values:

- » *Experiential* values involve something important to us. Love is perhaps the prime example of such a value. Frankl, clearly shaped by the experience of being separated from and eventually losing his wife, felt that love can go on without the beloved's presence; it is a connection with the loved one's inner self that can exist even after the beloved's death. He believed that the truest romantic love supersedes the sexual experience, as sex can be an expression of love but does not necessarily mean that love is present.

- » *Creative* values have to do with pursuing and participating in activities that challenge our minds: the arts, inventing, or other intellectual pursuits. Connection to creative values means participating in purposeful work throughout our lives.

- » *Attitudinal* values have to do with the ways in which we conceptualize events, and with how that conceptualization can spur us to acts of courage. In this scenario, we can find meaning even in suffering. For instance, grief is the ultimate conclusion of having been able to love in the first place. In that sense, Frankl stated, grief can help the meaning of love resonate more fully.

Frankl identified depression, addiction, and aggression as the three components of a **mass neurotic triad** that he saw as being caused by a fundamental lack of meaning or by misdirection in the search for meaning. Using data from various people troubled by these three challenges, Frankl showed that these people scored particularly low on measures meant to assess the strength of life purpose.

Frankl believed that even those of us actively trying to pursue our life's meaning can sometimes go off course. There are negative consequences for trying too hard (**hyperintention**) and for thinking too hard (**hyperreflection**). Sometimes we need to reframe a question entirely: Frankl believed that too often we are focused on what we should expect from life, when the real question is what life should expect from us.

With logotherapy, Frankl also originated some specific therapeutic tools, such as the use of **paradoxical intention**, whereby, for example, someone suffering from insomnia is encouraged to try to stay awake, or someone worried about inappropriately bursting into tears is encouraged to try actively to cry. This approach seems to overwrite the involuntary aspect of insomnia or crying, and it often shows that whatever is resisted or feared actually isn't so bad. The use of paradoxical intention makes people feel much more relaxed and in control. Frankl also saw great value in using humor as a way to help someone temporarily rise above the emotional difficulty of a given ordeal.

Frankl's writings and theories, infused with spirituality, sometimes seem to move from the realm of psychology into the world of morality and religion. In his writings, Frankl discusses transcendence in terms that involve a higher faith. This feature of his work can be seen as a strength or as a weakness, of course, but his overall focus on conscience—what truly guides our behavior, and how we achieve a purpose in life that is greater than ourselves—still resonates.

Frankl wrote that, no matter what is taken away from us, we are always free to choose our own attitude and our own way in any situation. This idea aligns him squarely with other psychology pioneers, across various schools of thought, who believed that it is our perception of things that matters, and that we have the capacity to grow and to change our perceptions. This idea becomes even more poignant when we imagine Frankl among hopeless, dying people in a concentration camp.

THEN WHAT?

Man's Search for Meaning remains a widely embraced book, and logotherapy went on to influence humanistic therapy and existential therapy directly. Various techniques from logotherapy have been incorporated into all kinds of schools of thought in psychology, including cognitive behavioral therapy. Frankl's thoughts on the nature of suffering have spurred inquiry in the field of philosophy as well.

WHAT ABOUT ME?

Frankl's ideas raise some provocative questions pertinent to modern life. Is suffering to be endured or eradicated? Is it always to be avoided, or can it be a gift in some forms?

Of course, the atrocities of the Holocaust are a horror whose magnitude defies understanding. But far less severe forms of suffering, both profound and mundane, may very well serve a purpose in our lives.

If you can bring yourself to do it, think back to some of your life's most painful moments. Not the time you had a kidney stone or got your hand stuck in the minivan door, but times of emotional pain and suffering. It is possible, of course, that you have dealt with chronic anxiety or depression. But outside those situations, it is likely that your suffering came down to a more singular event that could help spur you on in your quest for meaning. You need not be grateful that this event happened, of course. But it may have defined you as a person in a way that you came to recognize as having taught you something. Perhaps your most painful experience involved the death of a loved one. Why did it hurt so terribly? Frankl felt that the answer is clear: You felt that loss so deeply because you allowed yourself to love and be attached to this person. You were real in your connection with your lost loved one, and you were experiencing life fully. Similarly, your grief is a form of living and feeling as well. It means being alive and letting that person's previous existence still matter to you. Frankl once told a patient that grieving someone's death also means knowing that the loved one has been spared the pain of the loss that would have come if the grieving person had died first. Grieving also means engaging with life in all its forms. To run from it, mask it, or dull it does nothing helpful and provides only temporary relief. But finding meaning in grief, and fully living it, can ultimately help a person make it through.

The idea of suffering as a potential growth experience raises some controversial questions. Are we becoming too quick as a society to alleviate individual discomfort? Do we view fundamentally human experiences, such as mourning and grief, as medical problems to be summarily taken care of? Are we too fast to medicate, treat, and alleviate rather than let ourselves and others fully experience? Much controversy surrounded the recent decision that the fifth edition of the *Diagnostic and Statistical Manual of Mental Disorders* (*DSM-5*) would stop excluding people in bereavement from a diagnosis of depression. In other words, it used to be that if you had recently lost a loved one, depressive symptoms were considered normal and to be expected, and you weren't classified as having a disorder. That thinking has changed, in part because of the argument that providing grieving individuals with a diagnosis can help legitimize their suffering and perhaps improve their access to treatment. (Of course, the interests of pharmaceutical companies also align with higher diagnosis rates.) But the overall concern remains: If we continue to pathologize natural parts of human experience, are we ignoring and missing the ability of pain to help us grow?

In terms of some of Frankl's other theories, have you ever needed just to take a break from trying too hard or overfocusing on something? Perhaps you perseverated so much on a career or relationship quandary that you could barely stand to think about it (and your friends couldn't, either). You believed that thinking and self-reflection were good things, and yet you found yourself going nowhere—you rehashed and rehashed, and it didn't seem to help. You felt that you knew less than you did before, and you didn't feel motivated to move forward. It's classic paralysis by analysis, a case of hyperreflection. When contemplation starts to get in the way of actually living, you can stunt yourself. It is said that Socrates once declared the unexamined life not worth living. But it has also been pointed out that the unlived life is not worth examining. Frankl would likely argue that if you find yourself overanalyzing your next move so much that you get stuck, you are getting farther and farther away from finding meaning.

Albert Ellis

—●—●—

BORN 1913, Pittsburgh, Pennsylvania

DIED 2007, New York City, New York

Educated at the City University of New York and Columbia University

BIG IDEA

Albert Ellis began his adult life with a career in business administration and a dream of being a writer—a somewhat unlikely start to becoming one of the most influential psychologists of all time—but what started him on the latter path was his interest in theories of sexual relationships, which led him to put together a collection of essays, *The Case for Sexual Liberty*. As more and more people sought his advice after the publication of that book, he discovered that he really enjoyed counseling

people. He became an enthusiastic disciple of psychoanalysis and was accepted into a psychoanalytic training program without first earning a medical degree—a rarity at the time—and then went on to get a doctorate in psychology. After a few years in practice, however, he lost faith in some of the principles of psychoanalysis, and by 1957 he had written the book *How to Live with a Neurotic* and established what he called *rational therapy*, which eventually morphed into rational-emotive behavior therapy (REBT).

[handwritten note: → Cognitive Behavioral Therapy]

REBT is indeed quite different from psychoanalysis. The therapist in psychoanalysis tends to be rather passive, but an REBT therapist is encouraged to be active and to directly challenge a patient's unrealistic beliefs. REBT involves directly confronting patients' self-defeating patterns, helping them readjust their thinking and transform their cognitions into healthier, more adaptive ways of approaching the world. What Ellis established became the forerunner of cognitive therapy.

He also helped bridge the gap between psychotherapeutic treatment and scientific experimentation. Therapists were still overwhelmingly psychoanalytic, and experiments were still overwhelmingly behaviorist. By introducing more concrete, measurable techniques, Ellis became a pioneer in the search for quantifiable, empirically validated outcomes in psychotherapy.

REBT, in Ellis's words, has three components: A, B, and C, for *activating experiences*, *beliefs*, and *consequences*, respectively. Activating experiences are the circumstances that trigger an emotional reaction in someone: a trauma, a breakup, a stressful work environment. Beliefs are the thought systems that we develop as a result of our experiences; such thoughts are often self-sabotaging and irrational, and they are often responsible for our unhappiness. And consequences are often negative emotions—loneliness, anxiety, hope-lessness—that arise from our beliefs.

Ellis emphasized that it is not the activating experiences themselves but rather our beliefs about them that actu-ally cause our unhappiness and long-term patterns of dysfunction. Where treatment comes into play has to do with D and E: the therapist's *disputing* of such beliefs, and the therapist's help in encouraging

the patient to work toward the more positive *effects* of a new and healthier belief system. As for irrational beliefs themselves, Ellis identified many common ones. The most commonly damaging ones, he posited, are those that involve a perfectionistic attitude about how competent one must be, the conviction that others are terrible people if they don't always treat one considerately, and the demand that the world make one happy at all times. The therapist's job is to persistently question such beliefs. Four questions commonly come up:

» Is there evidence for this belief?
» Is there evidence against it?
» If you stop having this belief, what is the worst thing that can happen?
» If you stop having this belief, what is the best thing that can happen?

The therapist and the patient hash it out, and the patient gradually comes to understand the contradictions within such beliefs and adopts a more rational approach. Though Albert Ellis believed in the importance of self-acceptance, his objective approach extended to the very notion of the self—he was not inter-ested in more transcendent or actualized versions of the self, such as those that humanistic therapy tended to espouse.

Ellis's early interest in sexual theory never went away, and throughout his career he continued to write and conduct research on human sexual behavior. His 1958 book *Sex Without Guilt* is thought to be one catalyst of the American sexual revolution of the 1960s. He allowed his beliefs to evolve along with the times, gradually adopting a more accepting philosophy around same-sex relationships. His criticism of some of the effects of religion—especially as he felt some religious beliefs led to guilt and agitation—was another area in which he clashed occasionally with more conservative cultures.

Ellis himself seemed larger than life, with a rather abrasive though personable style in the therapy room, a further departure from previous styles of psychotherapy (but one that need not be a component of cognitive interventions). For the last 40 years of his life, he taught popular Friday seminars on therapeutic techniques, sometimes lacing them with profanity in a no-nonsense, humorous, confrontational way. In many respects, he was the anti-Freud: direct, action-oriented, and demystifying, believing that therapy shouldn't have to take years, and that it should be confrontational, transparent, make sense, and quit beating around the bush. He wrote more than 70 books that were accessible and aimed at laypeople, such as *How to Stubbornly Refuse to Make Yourself Miserable About Anything—Yes, Anything*.

THEN WHAT?

Ellis's techniques were a clear forerunner, along with Aaron Beck's work, of cognitive therapy and later cognitive behavioral therapy. Through a long career that continued until he died, when he was just short of 94 years old, Ellis was arguably the psychologist most responsible for moving therapy techniques into the realm of shorter-term, "face your problems" types of interventions. This had a tremendous impact on the public outside the therapy room as well, in terms of shaping cultural beliefs about self-help.

WHAT ABOUT ME?

It is easy at first glance to assume that REBT and its descendants merely tie a pretty bow around your life, encouraging you to look on the bright side or ignore adverse things that are happening. On the contrary, REBT is based on the premise that life will not always be fair and that some acceptance of negative things is necessary in order for you to become happier. So adversity is most definitely acknowledged. But an REBT therapist—or a good friend employing its techniques—will help you look at adversity in a different light, paving the way for you to become more optimistic and autonomous in actually being able to deal with it.

Let's imagine the case of a disheartening medical diagnosis. You find out that you have diabetes, and the significant lifestyle changes that will be required—along with the implications of having such an illness—are bringing down your mood and making you hopeless. REBT would urge you not to ignore your diagnosis or put yourself in denial with a vague "Everything will be okay." It would encourage you to face your diagnosis in a realistic, autonomous way. After a session or two of REBT, you might regard your diagnosis as a wake-up call and determine to work with your doctor to find specific strategies to help you not only cope with diabetes but also improve your overall health. This is not pie-in-the-sky thinking or avoiding the reality of the diagnosis. You would experience an improvement not only in your mood but also in your ability to move forward and cope with the challenge at hand.

Larger-scale beliefs can also be identified and challenged through these types of interventions. Ellis illuminated meaningful connections between particular beliefs and particular moods, and he worked with his patients to help them identify the antecedents and consequences of their behavior in systematic ways so that they could avoid sliding down the slippery slope from irrational thoughts to a depressed mood. Later cognitive therapists adopted Ellis's discoveries and techniques, such as the use of mood journals and logs of automatic thoughts. Albert Ellis understood that the more rigid and maladaptive we are in our beliefs, the more we defeat ourselves, and the higher the price we pay. What he gave his fellow psychotherapists was the gift of a blueprint for challenging irrational, maladaptive beliefs.

Aaron Beck

BORN 1921, Providence, Rhode Island

Educated at Brown University and Yale Medical School

BIG IDEA

Aaron Beck is a giant in the field whose work sits at the intersection of cognitive research and psychotherapy. In fact, many see him as the founder of cognitive therapy.

Beck began as a psychoanalyst and wanted to see how psychoanalysis could be helpful for depressed people. Discouraged by the lack of empirical evidence in this area, he was soon led to seek out more concrete and quantifiable types of interventions, and he began to focus on interventions that examine and even challenge specific ways of thinking. He developed cognitive therapy independently of Albert Ellis's work on rational-emotive behavior therapy, though both approaches overlap in their time frames.

Beck identified particular ways in which people who are depressed tend to think of themselves, their worlds, and their futures. Not surprisingly, their views tend toward the negative. But their thoughts also prove to be automatic—they are so ingrained that they're often taken as truth, without being the least bit challenged. The problem, as Albert Ellis showed, is that such thoughts are not necessarily aligned with reality, or even rational. They are examples of errors and distortions in thinking, and yet they rule the way depressed people see themselves and the world around them.

Beck's cognitive theory of depression says that such automatic thoughts and distorted interpretations are a fundamental part of being depressed, and that they represent a systematic bias in depressed people's thinking that serves to maintain and perpetuate their depression. But if such thoughts can be challenged and identified, then perhaps healthier patterns of thinking—and thus improvements in mood—can be attained.

Beck proposed that frequent negative thoughts often reflect a person's core beliefs. They are cognitive patterns, or **schemas** (**schemata**), that come from early experiences like being harshly criticized throughout childhood, losing a parent, or being rejected by peers. These core beliefs are neither helpful nor accurate, but they persist and are felt to be real and fundamental parts of life. And they tend to be self-fulfilling; the depressed person, believing that things will go badly, tends to create a set of circumstances that will indeed lead to things going badly.

Beck showed that additional **cognitive errors** are common among those who are depressed. **Arbitrary inferences** prompt people to make connections between things that are not really connected. And in **dichotomous thinking**, people see things in all-or-nothing or black-and-white terms. Overgeneralizing (blowing something out of proportion rather than seeing it as a specific, singular event) and paying selective attention to the negative (while tuning out the positive) are also patterns of thought frequently seen among those with depression. For Beck, every one of these cognitive errors represents a distortion that not only may contribute to the emergence of depressed thoughts but also may keep the depression from lifting later on.

Thankfully, Beck's development of cognitive therapy shows a way out of such thinking. The therapist's role is to challenge these thoughts in a caring way, illuminating just how irrational they are. These silent assumptions may never have been challenged before. This in turn will help a person learn to think more positively, creating automatic thoughts that are more realistic and adaptive. Positive thoughts will also be more goal-directed, making the person more active in ways that will solve problems and help him or her move forward, and making the self-fulfilling prophecy of failure less likely.

Beck also designed measures to assess symptomatology, so as to better quantify a person's progress in cognitive therapy. The Beck Depression Inventory has been used for decades to measure the signs and symptoms of depression in research settings as well as in clinical settings. Once again, the thinking is that breaking depression down into concrete thoughts, feelings, and behaviors promotes further understanding of what, exactly, depression consists of, and that this can help immensely with treatment. Beck's cognitive interventions have also been shown to have benefits beyond the treatment of depression. They have become implemented in standard treatment protocols for anxiety disorders, obsessive-compulsive disorders, and eating disorders as well.

THEN WHAT?

Beck directly influenced Martin Seligman, whose theories of depressed attributional styles and learned helplessness further expanded what we know about the depressed mind. Cognitive therapy created a completely new direction in treatment, leading to further therapies like cognitive behavioral therapy, which has branched out into additional formulations (including acceptance and commitment therapy) that are used to treat dozens of different psychological disorders.

WHAT ABOUT ME?

Let's say that you are walking down the street and you pass a colleague with whom you have been developing a friendship. The colleague seems to see you but doesn't acknowledge you at all. How do you interpret this situation? And how does it make you feel?

Some of us would come up with an explanation that doesn't involve negative thoughts about ourselves in the least: "Wow, she must not have seen me. She's probably distracted. Perhaps it wasn't her I saw at all, but someone who looks like her." But others among us—and most likely the ones most prone to depression—will make it not only all about us but also all about our presumed flaws: "She's embarrassed to say hello to me! She doesn't like me after all! I must have insulted her somehow!" Of course, in any given situation, the truth is still unknown, and it could fall anywhere along the spectrum of these two different ways of thinking. Yet depressed people systematically and chronically think in terms of negative interpretations that involve them, and such automatic negative thinking is likely both a cause and an effect of being depressed.

The other two fundamentally negative ways of thinking that Beck identified—about the world at large, and about one's future—can also be seen quite easily in the everyday lives of those who are depressed. If the roof on your newly built home starts leaking, do you view it as a specific problem, or do you think more generally that the entire house must be a dump? If you have an uncomfortable confrontation with your manager at work, do you quickly assume that you'll get fired? And if you do get fired, do you assume that your career is ruined and that you'll never find fulfilling work again? Beck's work further shows us that it is not what happens to us in life that determines our feelings. It is our interpretation of what happens that matters, along with how we carry these thoughts around with us.

Specific cognitive errors may be so common that you don't even notice them in yourself. Perhaps you're not even depressed, but you engage in all-or-nothing thinking. It seems to play a role in myriad ways of feeling bad, from anxiety and panic to low self-esteem, perfectionism, and hopelessness. Such dichotomous thinking locks you into a rigid way of seeing the world, and if that perspective is already negative, then the bad gets magnified

immensely: "My kid has been talking back sometimes—she's completely disrespectful!" "My boss put in one comment about me needing to be more prompt—I got an awful review!" "I had a second dessert—my diet is totally ruined!" All these thoughts represent cognitive leaps that are illogical and negative, and they will keep us on the path of feeling bad instead of finding ways to work toward our goals and overcome the initial problem. More realistic and adaptable methods of thinking could help us better address the challenges we face, be less angry and desperate about our kids' behavior, and feel less demoralized and awkward at work. Certainly, more realistic

and adaptable thinking can help us keep two desserts from turning into a dozen.

Maybe you have a friend or family member who is particularly good at playing devil's advocate and showing you the errors of your thinking, especially when you are mentally spinning out and getting down on yourself about a setback that you've experienced. That confidante, by playing the role of a gentle but firm interlocutor, is challenging your automatic thoughts and supporting you in restructuring them into more rational and less depressing ways of thinking that actually make sense and make you feel better. And that person has a lot in common with a cognitive therapist.

Carl Rogers

BORN 1902, Oak Park, Illinois

DIED 1987, San Diego, California

Educated at the University of Wisconsin and Teachers College, Columbia University

BIG IDEA

Carl Rogers was a clinician through and through. His research and writing made an indelible impact on psychology, but by all accounts his presence in the therapy room—genuine and warm—was also something to behold.

The approach that Rogers pioneered was originally called *person-centered psychotherapy* and eventually came to be known as **client-centered psychotherapy**. Both played a large role in

the founding of humanistic therapy. Rogers believed that people in pain did not need to be talked down to and did not need their distress pathologized. He showed that some of the most powerful therapeutic techniques don't have to be complicated; they are about simply being a caring person in the room. His approach underscores two ideas: that an effective therapist truly recognizes a person's potential, and that an effective therapist truly recognizes a person's capacity for lifelong growth. According to Rogers, among a therapist's most important responsibilities are conveying those ideas, being a supportive presence in the therapy room, and collaborating in the client's growth.

These ideas ran counter to the well-trod path of psychoanalysis, which has not been particularly concerned with being egalitarian. In fact, psychoanalysts call the people they treat *analysands* or *patients*, whereas humanistic therapy uses the more egalitarian term *clients*. Rogers saw the power dynamics of psychoanalysis as troubling and potentially manipulative. Psychoanalysis, Rogers argued, also overemphasizes the baggage of the past at the expense of recognizing a person's true and inspiring potential in the present. Despite his gentle manner in the therapy room, Rogers was not afraid of picking a fight with this older school of thought, and humanistic psychotherapy came to be known as the **third force**, a refreshing new wave after psychoanalysis and behaviorism.

Humanistic therapy's fundamental differences with behaviorism stem from humanistic therapy's emphasis on the potential for inner growth, as opposed to environmental conditioning. Rogers very much believed that we, not external stimuli or other people, are in charge of our own lives. In fact, Rogers and the behaviorist guru B. F. Skinner even appeared together for a series of debates: two giants in the field, hashing out their disparate beliefs and making history in the process.

So what does humanistic therapy actually look like? The hallmarks of Rogers's client-centered approach, outlined in *Client-Centered Therapy* (1951) and *On Becoming a Person* (1961), are the warm, empathetic presence of the therapist and the therapist's nondirective way of helping clients find and understand their true feelings, without the therapist's having undue influence on that process. The therapist is not to force issues but rather to create an environment ripe for self-exploration and inquiry. Rogers believed that people have a fundamental need to experience genuineness and an understanding ear, and that they are helped by having their feelings reflected back to them. And being nonjudgmental is key: Rogers believed that individuals have the capacity to correct their own mistakes when given the right supportive forum.

Another important tenet of Rogers's approach is **unconditional positive regard**: He posited that to feel truly accepted and cared for, no matter what, is an extremely powerful experience. His theory says that when people's self-worth is tied to conditions—certain achievements, saying the right thing, acting in a particular way—they suppress the deepest, truest parts of who they really are in order to fit themselves into the boxes that will gain them love and acceptance. It's not hard to imagine how this can lead to confusion, distress, and self-doubt. The gaps between the real self (who we are) and the ideal self (who we "should" be) can spur us to dislike ourselves, and Rogers felt that this happens to virtually all of us, to some degree. But being in the presence of someone who offers us true empathetic understanding, validating our feelings and even being willing to experience them along with us, can help us become whole and spur us toward real growth.

Despite the feel-good nature of humanistic therapy, Rogers's theories are neither subjective nor fuzzy. In fact, he pioneered new methods of doing research on the effectiveness of therapeutic techniques. It's rather astounding that, before Rogers, not many practitioners had really tried to do that in the decades since Freud's founding of psychoanalysis. Rogers prized the importance of empirical validation and sought objectivity in assessing the success of his therapeutic tools. He recorded sessions, provided transcripts, and broke the fundamentals of client-centered therapy down into concrete, teachable techniques. He was intent on demystifying the psychotherapeutic process and often displayed examples of his interventions, complete with a volunteer suffering from a real problem, to packed audiences. He called these presentations *demonstration interviews* and considered them genuine slices of the therapeutic relationship.

At the end of his life, Rogers had begun to apply his techniques to larger groups, including people outside the United States who were involved in racial or religious conflict. Such interventions took him to South Africa and Belfast. The realization that the benefits of a healing, person-to-person interaction could be extended to larger, starkly conflicted groups was an important breakthrough for our thinking about how psychotherapeutic techniques can help address society's problems as a whole.

THEN WHAT?

Rogers's humanistic approach—so widely used that it is often simply referred to as the Rogerian approach—has influenced generations of mental health practitioners and people in other helping professions, such as the ministry. His approach has even spread to business, encounter groups, conflict resolution, and sensitivity training. His emphasis on research also set the stage for decades of study on empirically validated treatment techniques.

WHAT ABOUT ME?

Let's say you have a friend who has asked to meet with you and talk about a crucial personal problem. If you receive these requests with any frequency, chances are you have learned to be an empathetic listener—making eye contact, offering nonjudgmental and understanding statements, and asking, "How have you thought about handling it?" instead of announcing, "Here's what you should do." Even without realizing it, you are probably taking the Rogerian approach, which says that in order to really help people, you should be there in the moment, connect with what they're feeling, and even share their feelings to some extent. When people know that you respect and love them without conditions, you can help them make their best choices and be their best selves.

As a clinical psychologist in private practice, I often talk on the phone for about 30 minutes with a potential client who is in emotional pain. I take some history, assess the person's level of distress, answer questions, and determine whether we will be a good fit and what our goals will be. If everything is a go, then we schedule our first in-person session. But most of the time, something very interesting happens between the phone call and the first session: The potential client almost always experiences a lift in mood, which often takes the form of a reduction in symptoms and a sense that things aren't as bad as they seemed. Is it the magic of my phone voice? Nope. It's the theories of Carl Rogers playing out in real life. I gave the person hope. I let the potential client know that we were in it together. I showed the person that I cared, that I would be there, and that he or she had value to me. I listened and didn't judge. I accepted and validated the person's emotional experience and showed that I would not shy away from it. Whether the client is suffering from depression or disordered eating or anxiety or any number of other problems, we still have much work to do. But we've already connected as human beings—and the beautiful importance of that fact is Carl Rogers's greatest legacy.

Virginia Satir

●—●

BORN 1916, Neillsville, Wisconsin

DIED 1988, Menlo Park, California

Educated at the University
of Wisconsin and the University
of Chicago

BIG IDEA

A social worker, Virginia Satir was a pioneer of family therapy. She fundamentally changed the way we think about the family unit and its role both in creating mental health problems and in healing them.

Many of Satir's treatment techniques were researched and developed at the Mental Research Institute in Palo Alto, California, an organization she was involved with since its founding in 1959. Earlier in her career, when she was in private practice, she had noticed how helpful it is to bring family members into an individual's treatment process. In 1962, she became the institute's training director for the first-ever family therapy training program. Satir believed that it's rare for a person's suffering to exist in a vacuum, and that it is commonly related to issues within the family environment. Unlike previous therapists, who might simply have blamed a parent's past behavior for a client's current problems, she believed that troubled relationships from the past can be worked on in the present. In some cases, she felt, perhaps there isn't even an individual problem at all but rather a problem in the way that individuals fit together.

Satir's family therapy took many forms, from providing family members with basic communication techniques to creating a safe space for family members to face and explore deep pain and trauma. All her interventions focused on accepting and understanding the present and on working toward growth and change. Satir, like practitioners of humanistic therapy, believed that people are capable of this throughout the life span. She pioneered therapeutic techniques like role-playing and even established family camps, where families' treatment took place over a weekend or longer in nature. Over time, Satir began to see the family as a microcosm, and she believed that techniques and philosophies from family treatment can be applied to the world at large.

Satir was also particularly interested in the importance of self-esteem. She was an early explorer of in-the-moment techniques like affirmations and visualization, and she was also a proponent of meditation. Her short 1975 book *Self-Esteem* reads almost like poetry, beginning with "I am me. In all the world, there is no one else like me." It's been embraced for decades by those seeking to accept themselves with all their flaws and find the motivation to continue growing.

Satir's therapy techniques also emphasize, in practical terms, the difference between the **presenting problem** (insomnia, irritability, dating problems, clashes with a boss) and underlying challenges that may actually be more important (depression, trauma, dysfunctional relationship patterns). It is up to the therapist, Satir said, to help people discover and understand the connections between the problems they bring to therapy and the more fundamental issues that may be at the root of their suffering.

Satir also recognized that science can develop all the treatment techniques under the sun, but if people aren't able to access them, those techniques will do no good. She pushed for the creation of therapy networks to help train providers and spread treatment into places where it hadn't been accessible before. Indeed, Satir's techniques spread globally, and by the end of her life, she was training practitioners around the world. She was a teacher through and through, and family therapy—its importance, how to do it, and what could be gained from it—was the area of her greatest lessons.

THEN WHAT?

Many different styles of family therapy have grown from Satir's work, and the fact that it's since become a specialty in its own right, with certain therapists doing nothing else, speaks to the demand for it and to its importance within treatment. The Satir Change Process Model has extended the constructs of growth and change into management and is used in business.

WHAT ABOUT ME?

Imagine that one of your best friends comes to you with complaints about her marriage. She feels frustrated and taken for granted, and she says that her husband has expressed annoyance that she is on his back about household tasks. She says she's beginning to get depressed about it, and that her husband seems more and more irritable. You know your friend and her husband well, and you like them both on an individual basis very much. You also know that they have a strong love for each other, carry a meaningful history together, and share parenting roles for their two young children. You participated in their wedding and have always seen them as a couple who can go the distance; you look up to them and admire the characteristics they each bring to their marriage.

What is their diagnosable problem? Is either of them, individually, doing anything wrong? Individually or together, are they necessarily suffering from some sort of psychological dysfunction or behaving in ways that are self-sabotaging or unhealthy? In short, can two psychologically healthy people be in a psychologically unhealthy relationship? And can this happen within families?

The answer is yes, absolutely. In the preceding scenario, you would probably urge your friends to work their problems out, encouraging them to consider seeing a counselor together. You would try not to take sides and would abstain from pathologizing their behavior. You'd probably try to help them understand that they could use some help with their communication patterns and with working on their daily expectations of one another. The notion that neither of them is necessarily wrong, but that instead it is their dynamic that may need some work, is one that we take for granted now. But the wide acceptance of this idea grew directly from Virginia Satir's early work.

We could take this example even further, to reflect an additional area of Satir's interest. Let's say it turns out that your friend's mother died last year, and that your friend's mother sacrificed a lot to raise her family because she belonged to a generation that dictated motherhood as the limit of a woman's ambitions. Your friend is not only grieving but also reevaluating her own life—worrying and overanalyzing her own choices and sacrifices, wondering if she'll someday have the same regrets her mother had, ruminating over having long ago made the decision not to go to law school, resenting her husband every time he so much as forgets to put a plate in the dishwasher. Of course, she won't mention any of this when she and her husband first see a counselor, because she won't yet have faced these underlying issues herself. Instead, she will report on the more superficial issue of being taken for granted by her husband. But a skilled therapist, one like Virginia Satir, will get to the underlying problem sooner rather than later.

Cognitive Psychology

The brain is, when all is said and done, a thinking apparatus. Almost every phrase in our language that refers to the brain recognizes this without equivocation, from "the brains of the operation" to "being brainy" (or, less favorably, "a birdbrain"). You don't tend to first think of your brain as a feeling organ, even though the experience of emotion is arguably just as important as thinking. Nor do you tend to think of the brain's primary role as influencing behavior, even though, as discussed at length in the section on Behavioral Psychology, it most certainly does that, too. For better or for worse, when we think of our brains, our primary association is that they are the headquarters for thought.

And it's thought itself that fascinates cognitive psychologists. How, specifically, do our thoughts come about? What gives rise to them, changes them, and allows them to influence our emotions and behavior in such significant ways? How does our brain create memories, and how do we make judgments about things, from what we want for dinner to whom we trust more as a political candidate? What is the role of intelligence, what really goes on internally during learning, and how are thoughts connected to moods, habits, and disordered behavior? Thoughts—cognitions, if you're feeling fancy—go hand in hand with virtually all aspects of our experience. They are fundamental aspects of our awareness and consciousness. Within the field of psychology, probably no one has thought more about thoughts than cognitive psychologists.

Alfred Binet

●━━●

BORN 1857, Nice, France

DIED 1911, Paris, France

Educated at the Sorbonne and at the Salpêtrière Hospital

BIG IDEA

Alfred Binet was a pioneer of intelligence testing, and some versions of intelligence tests used today—more than a century later—still bear his name. By most accounts, his interest in mental assessment and individual differences was sparked by the growth and development of his two daughters, who were two years apart.

At the time of Binet's work, other individual intelligence tests existed; Francis Galton and James McKeen Cattell had developed their own measures. But with

Binet's research, intelligence testing moved ahead in leaps and bounds, as did the conceptualization of intelligence as a more general attribute that could be represented by performance across multiple spheres.

The need to perform large-scale assessments of intelligence became particularly pronounced with the advent of compulsory attendance within the French public school system. School officials wanted to identify children who could not keep up, to see if they should be sent to special schools or special programs. It was Binet who was selected to meet this challenge. In 1905, he presented his first test, consisting of 30 tasks across a wide range of difficulties. Behaviors to be measured included everything from the ability to follow a light with the eyes (on the easier end of the spectrum) to extremely difficult sentence-completion tasks. The goal was for this to be an objective and empirical way to identify children who were slower learners, and who perhaps even had significant intellectual deficits.

What began to set Binet's tests apart over time was their usage of norms, or averages of wide ranges of data. The more people who were tested, the more data was collected. And with more data came a more solid foundation that would give any individual result greater context and meaning. Imagine that you and two of your coworkers have a competition to see who can remember the longest string of numbers. Whether you rank first, second, or third, you necessarily gain a particularly insightful assessment of where you stand in terms of memory. After all, what if your coworkers are geniuses—or amnesiacs? Now let's imagine instead that the same memory assessment is standardized and administered to 10,000 people, a wide range of American adults. Now your ranking—which shows you where you stand in comparison to not just 2 but 9,999 others—seems much more useful, doesn't it?

So Binet gradually extended the length of his tests, and he increasingly tweaked them to reflect the research he was doing. Over time, he amassed a set of norms for performance across a wide range of ages, and this allowed him to identify intelligence levels with much more precision than if someone just had particularly noticeable deficits and needed special schooling. Ultimately, Binet developed a way of comparing any

individual child's performance to that of an "average" child of that age group. Copying a drawing, recognizing coins and making change, noticing absurdities in language—Binet's test assessed different areas of mental functioning, with the overall score thought to provide a meaningful big picture of a person's general intelligence. Binet's results were lent further validity when it was shown how closely they matched teachers' own assessments of their students' intellectual capacity.

The tasks within the test formed a ladder, with individual rungs for individual subtests. And how far a child could ascend on the ladder would theoretically be reflective of his intelligence level and would be considered to be his or her mental age. Intelligence, Binet believed, continued to develop with age until maturity was reached. Later, William Stern pioneered the idea of the intelligence quotient (IQ), which, in its most rudimentary form, was a comparison of a person's mental age with his or her actual chronological age.

Binet felt that a child should be compared only to other children of similar background, as he recognized that both genetics and environment likely contributed to overall intelligence. Eventually his tests were extended to include adults, shaping the role of psychological measurement for a century and counting.

THEN WHAT?

Binet's original tests eventually morphed into the Binet-Simon Scale, as amended by his student Theodore Simon. They then made their way to the United States, where Lewis Terman incorporated them into the Stanford-Binet Intelligence Scales, a test that, in its fifth edition, is still given today. Binet's focus on the quantitative measurement of intelligence, and on psychological assessment in general, opened up a new field of inquiry regarding the quantification of psychological characteristics. Binet's findings within cognitive development also influenced notable developmental psychologists, including Jean Piaget. Binet's contributions created a niche for psychological measurement to help solve real-world problems. And though he predated the behaviorists, Binet's empirical approach foreshadowed their beliefs about the importance of precise quantification.

WHAT ABOUT ME?

Perhaps you have truly known your relative intellectual strengths and weaknesses since you were a young child. But you might be surprised. What you think you're good at may not necessarily be what you're actually good at, or maybe you think you're more or less intelligent than you really are. But what is intelligence, exactly? We tend to think of being smart as one characteristic rather than as a complicated collection of characteristics. Even if you are just talking about mental strength and abilities—ignoring all the other multiple types of intelligence

that were conceptualized after Binet, like emotional intelligence, athletic intelligence, artistic intelligence, and so on—it may be surprising that there are still so many different ways to be intelligent. The person who won the spelling bee in middle school, the person who is a math whiz, the person who can solve the Rubik's Cube without fail—are those people necessarily smart across the board?

If you have ever taken an intelligence test with subscales, like Binet's, it can be fascinating to compare your relative strengths and weaknesses. How is your visual-spatial reasoning? Are you someone who can figure out immediately how to fit all your family's different suitcases into the back of your SUV? Or are you someone who gets all the way to the end of the IKEA instructions without once realizing that the large piece off to the side should have been used in an earlier step in order for the dresser to fit together correctly?

What about your working memory, the brain's clipboard function? Perhaps you just changed your password (for the nineteenth time) five minutes ago, but now, when you are trying to log in on a different device, you can't remember it. Sound familiar? Good working memory allows us to calculate how much we've accrued on our bar tab, keep driving directions in mind as we proceed, or remember the names of the two new people we just met while we're still in conversation with them. And these abilities vary vastly among people.

Let's take quantitative reasoning. It involves math, of course, but it's not necessarily synonymous with having memorized your multiplication tables up to 20, or knowing the exact formula for figuring out the cosine of a triangle. Instead, quantitative reasoning involves a natural aptitude for solving problems in numerical terms. Are you someone who automatically and intuitively understands that on your 30th birthday you're not starting your 30th year but rather your 31st? (After all, in your first year, as a baby, you were not yet 1.) Were you always very good at those contests that asked you to name the number of gumballs in a gumball machine, and are you great at quickly comparing which football stadium will seat more people? If so, you may very well have good quantitative reasoning abilities, even if you never paid attention in math class.

Of course, when we are distracted, stressed, sleep-deprived, or depressed, our concentration and ability to think and remember can be significantly compromised. This can also be true during the actual taking of the intelligence test.

In some people, discrepancies in capabilities across the different intelligence subtypes are so pronounced as to constitute a learning disability in those domains where they perform especially poorly. Someone can be intellectually gifted in one area, but relative deficits in another area create a striking contrast. Such assessments are very commonly given to children whose parents or teachers have a concern. Identifying these relative differences early on can often help with the creation of a personalized plan for someone's learning to be maximized. That really brings things full circle, back to Binet's testing origins of more than a century ago, when testing was used to help figure out how to meet the needs of French schoolchildren.

Ulric Neisser

BORN 1928, Kiel, Germany

DIED 2012, Ithaca, New York

Educated at Harvard University and
Swarthmore College

BIG IDEA

Ulric (Dick) Neisser is considered by many
to be the founder of cognitive psychology.
His two most famous works—*Cognitive
Psychology*, from 1967, and *Cognition and
Reality*, from 1976—set the stage for a new
focus on the measurement and science of
thoughts and memories and were considered an important nail in the coffin of
behaviorism as the sole explanation of why
we act in the ways we do.

Though philosophers and early psychologists had been speculating on the
nature of thought for many centuries,
cognitive psychology brought thought into
the realm of the laboratory. That mental
processes, just like behavior, could be
measured with specificity was an important idea that began to take hold as the
study of cognitive psychology took off.
Neisser ushered in an era of new developments in scientific ways to observe,
assess, and quantify cognitive processes,
and the field of psychology, as a result,
was able to bid farewell to the limitations
of theoretical analysis and introspection
as the only ways to understand what,
exactly, goes on in our thought processes.

Neisser developed a specialty in the
domain of memory. He theorized that a
memory is not an exact, static snapshot
of a moment in time but rather an after-
the-fact mental reconstruction of an event.
That memory itself may be subject to all

kinds of psychological idiosyncrasies is an extremely important concept, as it opens the door to studying just how inaccurate our recall can be and to discovering what we can try to do about it. It also fundamentally changes the way we think about memory—the circumstances of the recollection may be just as important as the circumstances in which the memory itself was formed. Our minds are not perfect recorders, and we likely remember our memories of an event more than we remember the event itself. Inaccuracies easily seep in. Neisser showed that the process of formulating a memory and the context of how we remember are just as psychologically salient as the original experience of the remembered event.

Neisser viewed memory and experience as parts of an interactive cycle. He said that our schemas, or schemata, which are the mental structures we use to understand and organize our environment, directly affect our behavior. And, in turn, the experiences that we have go on to further modify our schemas. These processes repeat themselves in an infinite loop.

Neisser's most noteworthy work involved so-called **flashbulb memories**. That term refers to those iconic memories we have of the most significant and emotionally charged moments of our lives, and they are usually very potent. It was previously thought that the brain, during one of these emotional events, acted immediately to solidly imprint those important seconds and minutes into memory. But Neisser challenged this

notion, hypothesizing that what makes us remember flashbulb memories more clearly is the telling and retelling of the story of our experience, and that flashbulb memories are not inherently different from or stronger than everyday memories. He supported this idea with solid data demonstrating that flashbulb memories, though very strong and detailed, are actually not particularly accurate.

Neisser coined the term **repisodic memory**, wordplay on **episodic memory**. Episodic memory is autobiographical in nature: Where did you spend your 21st birthday? **Semantic memory** has to do with those facts and knowledge that we learn but that don't directly involve our own experience: Name five state capitals! But repisodic memory has to do with events that never really happened but that we seem to recall anyway. Such events, which we have somehow created in our minds, are typically very similar to events that have happened often to us, and so they don't actually come out of nowhere. Are we making them up? No. But they conform enough to our schemas—the general ideas we have of things that have happened to us—that they seem to fit in, and so we fill in the gaps of our recollections and construct these quasi-fake memories. Sometimes, Neisser showed, we can also commit the error of taking a group of events and blending them into a single memory.

Finally, Neisser did particularly interesting work on selective attention and perception, showing that when we are not paying particular attention to something, not only will we likely not remember it, we also might not even notice major and unusual aspects of it in the first place. Therefore, contextual factors affect not only our memories but also our entire perception of the remembered moment in the first place.

THEN WHAT?

Neisser's research on memory directly inspired later memory researchers, such as Elizabeth Phelps, who further explored the interaction of emotion and memory, and later longitudinal studies on flashbulb memory, such as an ongoing one about 9/11, which Phelps and many others are involved in. Neisser's having established the foundation of cognitive psychology as a field led to the additional multidisciplinary fields of behavioral neuroscience (which combines biological findings with cognitive psychology) and cognitive science (which extends beyond psychology to encompass linguistics, philosophy, and computer science).

WHAT ABOUT ME?

You likely have a collection of flashbulb memories stored within your brain from various times throughout your life. Some might be moments whose importance was significant to millions of others: the assassination attempt on President Ronald Reagan; the death of Michael Jackson; the terrible news of September 11, 2001.

Others might be more personal: when you proposed to your spouse; when you found out you had made partner at your law firm; when you got the call that your father had suffered a heart attack. Whether the memory in question is strictly personal or societally shared, it is quite likely that you have told the story multiple times of where you were or what you were doing at that pivotal moment, and that you began to tell your story not long after the experience itself. Talking about shared experiences of the same life-defining moment can often bring people together.

But though you may very well feel that the event is burned into your memory, and that each retelling has merely reconveyed those exact, never-changing details to a different audience, have you ever stopped to think that each time you retell the story, you might drift farther and farther away from the truth? Perhaps, for certain audiences, you omit certain facts or even add key details. And the next time you tell it, the story shifts ever so slightly, not because you are lying but because you are reconstructing the narrative as you recall it from the previous time.

Perhaps you've even had the surreal experience of finding an old journal and getting to reread your original account of an event soon after it occurred. You may have been startled and even embarrassed to see just how differently you've been recalling events over the years, no matter how you actually perceived them at the time. Of course, there can be a fine line between honest errors in memory

KEY EXPERIMENT Neisser's best-known experiment, published in 1992, explored the accuracy of flashbulb memories via college students' recollections of the space shuttle *Challenger* disaster. In 1986, the day after the tragedy, Neisser had 106 college undergraduates fill out a survey that asked the respondents where they were when they heard about the event, how they found out about it, whom they were with, what they were doing, and what time it was. Given that it was so soon after the occurrence, these accounts were taken to be a baseline, probably accurate recollections of the events as they happened. Just under three years later, the same students were given a fresh copy of the survey (44 were completed in total) and were also asked to rate how confident they were of their recollections. Only 7 percent of the students showed perfect recall; 68 percent produced combinations of accurate and inaccurate recollections; and 25 percent had recollections that were completely inaccurate. All in all, over 90 percent of the students' memories contained at least one major inaccuracy. And, most damning, the students with the completely inaccurate memories had the same high level of confidence as the students with the completely accurate ones. When the respondents were shown the two surveys together and were faced with the discrepancies, not one of them remembered the event more clearly or reverted to his or her earlier responses. Though the respondents were often somewhat upset by the differences in the stories they had told at two different points in time, they still tended to cling to their false memories.

and tendentious misrecollections that come from the desire to tell a story in a grandiose or self-serving way. Recall the controversy surrounding Brian Williams of NBC. He often repeated claims of having ridden in a military helicopter in Iraq that was forced down after having been hit by a rocket-propelled grenade. In January 2015, he told the story one time too many, as it was heard and challenged by people who had been involved in the actual incident, and who explained that the helicopter that was hit was the one that had been flying in front of the helicopter in which Williams was riding, and that his helicopter had not been directly involved. Though he was immediately suspended and eventually lost his role as a nightly news anchor, Williams has never clearly acknowledged that there was a deliberate attempt to tell the story differently from how he believed its events

had really occurred. His apologies have been along the lines of "I told stories that were wrong" or "I got the story wrong." And though additional discrepancies in some of his other reported stories have since come to light, it is hard to be certain that he actually lied. Looking back at his statements over years of retelling the helicopter incident, what you see is a gradual shift in how the story was told, with successive accounts placing him closer and closer to the heart of the action. Was this an egotistical attempt to stretch the truth? Was he riding the slippery slope of pushing the story to be more and more exciting, and continuing to get away with it? Or was it an inaccurate flashbulb memory that gradually drifted away from the real experience? Perhaps there was a little bit of both.

Albert Bandura

BORN 1924, Mundare,
Alberta, Canada

Educated at the University of British
Columbia and the University of Iowa

BIG IDEA

Albert Bandura's theories have spanned
social psychology, cognitive psychology,
personality psychology, and even psychotherapy. He is best known as the originator
of **social learning theory**, which puts
forth the idea that much of our behavior—
including aggression—is learned through
modeling and imitation. He later came to
call this *social cognitive theory*. His theory
is one of reciprocal determinism, with the
environment causing our behavior and
our behavior also influencing the environment. An individual's personality, Bandura

theorizes, is the product of the interaction
of environment, behavior, and cognitive
processes.

While the behaviorists emphasized
the need for reinforcement to exist in
order for a behavior to be performed or
repeated, Bandura has observed that we
often initiate behaviors even if we are
not being directly rewarded. Instead, we
may be imitating behaviors we have seen
performed by someone else. According
to Bandura, such **social modeling**
has four components: attention, retention, reproduction, and motivation.

The meaning of attention is clear: In
order for us to observe something in the
first place, we must be paying attention to
it. The level of attention we give something
can, of course, be affected not just by our
own variables (Are we tired? Preoccupied?
Upset?) but also by the variables of the

behavior we are observing, and of who is performing it: Does the person stand out? Is he attractive? Is she competent? Do we think of her as similar to ourselves? All of those factors make it more and more likely that we will pay attention.

The next step is retention: the process of actually recording and recalling what it is we have observed. We might create our own version of mental notes to categorize and summarize this behavior for later use.

Reproduction is the actual imitation that occurs, and this will depend on our abilities. It would likely take just one attempt for you to imitate someone turning a doorknob, whereas it might takes weeks of practice to imitate someone flipping a perfect pancake. And certain behaviors—performing gracefully in Zumba class, anyone?—might be forever outside your abilities.

The final component of modeling behavior, according to Bandura, is motivation. The behaviorists, of course, thought that motivation causes learning. Bandura says that we can learn through observation alone, but that motivation is necessary in order for us to imitate. This motivation can take the form of positive reinforcement or of punishment. But what sets social learning theory further apart is Bandura's argument that not just past reinforcement or punishment but also the promise of future reinforcement or punishment—and even vicarious reinforcement or punishment, which involves simply watching someone else be rewarded or punished—can serve as motivators. Like the behaviorists, Bandura acknowledges that positive reinforcement is typically more effective than punishment.

Bandura's most groundbreaking experiments have involved the motivation to act in aggressive ways. He showed that simply witnessing someone acting aggressively can spur on our own aggressive behavior. But if the temptation to model aggression is all around us, how do we ever learn to regulate our behavior? Bandura hypothesizes that the processes involved in self-regulation are self-observation, judgment, and self-response. We look at our behavior, we assess it in comparison to the behavior of others, and we determine how we should reward or punish ourselves. Related to this is Bandura's concept of **self-efficacy**, that is, the effect of our believing that we can be effective in a certain situation and can enact a desired behavior. This concept is distinct from the concepts of self-esteem and self-worth, both of which have to do with more general attitudes about our value as individuals.

Finally, Bandura has worked to develop types of therapy in which social modeling is put to good use. **Self-control therapy** involves overcoming habits by creating behavior charts that make you closely examine the details of your actions, creating contracts with yourself, and altering your environment in ways that will help you along in modifying your behavior patterns.

KEY EXPERIMENT Bandura's Bobo doll experiment (1961) and its follow-ups are among psychology's most famous, and they suggest that aggressive behavior is very frequently imitated. (A Bobo doll, by the way, a popular toy of the era, was an inflatable vinyl clown several feet tall with a weighted bottom, which meant that after Bobo was punched, he would quickly bounce back to an upright position.) The participants were 36 male and 36 female pre-schoolers at Stanford University's nursery school. The children were over the age of 3.5 years but under the age of 6 and were assessed beforehand for their baseline levels of natural aggressiveness. (It is worth noting that their race, ethnicity, and socioeconomic class were not recorded, and it is often assumed that Bandura's participants were overwhelmingly white and from a relatively high socioeconomic class, assumptions that have been the basis of some of the criticisms leveled against his findings. Later researchers have also criticized the study for not considering whether a given child was familiar with the Bobo doll and have suggested that such familiarity, or its absence, might have affected the level of the children's aggressiveness toward the doll.)

The original experiment had three groups of children and three conditions: children who were shown an aggressive interaction, children who were shown a nonaggressive interaction, and a control group of children who were shown no interaction at all. The groups were equally split, with 24 children (12 girls and 12 boys) in each. In addition, the experiment used a matched-pairs design, whereby children with similar levels of baseline aggressiveness were paired as they went through the experiment.

The children who were shown an aggressive interaction saw a male or female adult actor (called a *behavior model*) behave violently toward a Bobo

In **modeling therapy**, patients with specific fears watch other people modeling the behavior of overcoming their own fears, as when someone who at first is terrified of a snake gradually makes his way toward it and eventually even drapes it around his neck.

THEN WHAT?

Bandura's theories—part of the cognitive revolution that has emphasized the role that interpretation of an external event plays in the motivation to behave in certain ways—helped dethrone behaviorism as doll for about 10 minutes. The behavior models were physically as well as verbally aggressive, with various ways of attacking the doll—saying "Pow!" or "Sock him!" or "Boom!" and throwing it up in the air or even attacking it with a hammer. The children who were shown a nonaggressive interaction saw a male or female adult actor playing with Tinker Toys near the doll but not interacting with it. And the children in the control group, of course, saw no behavioral model or interaction at all. In controlled conditions after these witnessed interactions, Bandura found that the children who had observed the aggressive interaction were far more aggressive themselves and were prone to imitate the specific behaviors they had witnessed with the Bobo doll. Boys were more likely to favor imitating a same-sex behavior model than girls were. Boys imitated more physically aggressive acts than girls did, but there was no sex difference for verbal aggression. In a later version of this experiment, Bandura had children witness aggression on the part of real-life behavior models, human film models, and film cartoon (cat) models and found that children who had seen any of these models behaving aggressively were later, in the same controlled conditions, significantly much more likely than the children in the control group to behave aggressively themselves. Bandura also looked at whether seeing the model punished, rewarded, or not responded to at all influenced the children's later aggressive behavior. He found that it did not affect their learning of the aggressive behavior (the children could still demonstrate what they had seen), but it did affect their motivation to perform it on their own (when models were rewarded, the children were more likely to imitate the aggressive behavior spontaneously).

the predominant school of thought in psychology. His approach to observing behavior has greatly contributed to social psychology and even influenced personality theory. As a result, many now consider him one of the greatest living psychologists.

WHAT ABOUT ME?

Naturally, there is a lot of controversy about the nature of aggression and how easily it is modeled—especially in our modern age of not just watching violence, but also being able to participate in simulated versions of it through video games.

For every study (and there have been plenty since Bandura's) that suggests that we are more likely to act aggressively after watching aggression—and thus more likely to act violently after being exposed to violence—there is someone who gets defensive. But what personalized anecdotes ("Video games never hurt *me*!") fail to account for is that nowhere in any study's findings is it implied that every single person in every single real-life circumstance will exhibit exactly the same effects of being exposed to violence. Like most other research, studies on aggression are about probabilities. They don't purport to determine the exact nature of you or your life or your temperament or your experiences. They merely look for general trends in the data. Not everyone who smokes gets cancer; not everyone who drives without a seatbelt gets killed in a car accident. But that doesn't take away from what we know about the importance of those risk factors. Think about the habits we pick up through observation—phrases we use because a friend did, clothes we wear because they looked great on a model, sports we took up because our dads played them in high school. And the negatives— curse words we learned on the school bus, racist attitudes we absorbed from our grandparents, a habit of making fun of overweight people because our sisters did. We intuitively accept that many of our behaviors are learned because of our loved ones, our social influences, and our culture. There's no reason to assume that aggressive behavior would be an exception to this rule, but because aggression is a loaded subject, it is sometimes hard to talk about without a high level of emotion.

The concept behind modeling therapy is also something that resonates with our daily lives. "If I can do it, you can do it!" your friend might say when she starts to train for a 5K run, and when you watch how she starts slow, fits running into her schedule, and gradually increases her distances, you may deduce that you, too, can run such a race. "You go first," you might say to your brother when the two of you come across a particularly scary roller coaster at an amusement park, and then you watch from below as he gives you the thumbs-up on the second hill. In both situations, observing others—especially someone you consider to be like you—can pave the way for you to take on a new or feared challenge. Of course, if your friend is a triathlete and fitness model, her encouragement to you might not mean much. But, as Bandura found, if you consider someone to be like you, you pay more attention and are more likely to imitate that person's behavior. It's the fact that someone presumably has fears just like yours and is able to overcome them that makes that person a particularly effective cheerleader.

Elizabeth Loftus

●━●

BORN 1944, Los Angeles, California

Educated at Stanford University
and the University of California,
Los Angeles

BIG IDEA

A specialist in memory, Elizabeth Loftus
began her studies by looking at how
semantic memory is structured (recall
that semantic memory has to do with the
storage and recollection of impersonal
facts). While delving into the nuances of
how such memories are stored, Loftus was
struck by the need to better apply her findings to the world at large. And thus began
her interest in eyewitness testimony.

Loftus completely overturned the
way we think of eyewitness testimony. It
was already understood that memories
are reconstructed upon recall and are
subject to various biases, but Loftus
was able to show that being exposed to
misinformation—especially in the form
of leading questions—can alter and distort
memories considerably. This **misinformation effect**, though admittedly
disheartening, is arguably among the
most important discoveries of cognitive
psychology over the past several decades.

That false memories can be developed
because of misinformation conveyed by
someone else is something that hit home
for Loftus personally. Her mother drowned
in a swimming pool when Loftus was 14,
and when Loftus was in her 40s, an uncle
told her that she had been the one to find
her mother's body. Loftus had never had
many specific memories of that experience, but she felt them coming back to
her rather clearly over the days following

her uncle's revelation. Soon afterward, however, Loftus's brother called to tell her that her uncle had been mistaken. Loftus was alarmed to see her work playing out so personally—she saw firsthand how a false memory of a traumatic event can apparently be implanted. (Note that false memories don't involve inaccurately remembering certain events. Rather, they involve believing in the reality of events that never actually occurred. Someone falsely remembering an event can feel certain of its reality and quite earnest in his or her insistence that the event took place, regardless of all evidence to the contrary.)

Loftus's various experiments have shown how even subtle changes in the way a question about an event is worded can lead to a false memory. For example, after someone has viewed a video of a car accident, the question "Did you see *the* broken headlight?" is far more likely

to elicit memories of a broken headlight (even when there was no broken headlight in the video) than the question "Did you see *a* broken headlight?" Similarly, asking "How fast were the cars going when they smashed together?" will yield speed estimates significantly higher than "How fast were the cars going when they hit each other?" And the "smashed together" phrase will even yield false memories of broken glass, which is not in the video at all.

Even though some memories of abuse, for example, may be false, real cases of abuse, of course, do exist. In fact, one can realistically surmise that an inordinate number of abuse cases go unreported and even unspoken, and that they may greatly outnumber falsely recovered memories. But the sensitivity of these subjects has imbued Loftus's work with a great deal of controversy, as she has also testified at some high-profile cases, including those involving Ted Bundy, the Menéndez Brothers, the Hillside Strangler, and the Oklahoma City bombers. Victims' advocates and survivors of abuse have sometimes vilified Loftus because they believe that she is invalidating their experiences. But let's be clear: The fact that Loftus has identified the potential, under certain circumstances, for false memories to be generated does not negate the true stories of abuse survivors, nor does her work imply that those who have reported what have turned out to be false memories were actively and purposefully lying. What Loftus's work highlights, perhaps more than anything else, is just how unreliable the most emotional and traumatic memories can be.

THEN WHAT?

Elizabeth Loftus's work has had an immense impact outside academia, most specifically on how eyewitness testimony is viewed in criminal cases. A great many convictions that were later overturned because of DNA evidence have involved eyewitness testimony. Loftus's work has led to a new level of scrutiny in cases involving recovered memories, and it has inspired further research into the fragility and fallibility of human memory.

WHAT ABOUT ME?

Think back to your earliest memory. Were you 2? 5? 10? What is it, exactly, that you recall? Let's say it was a birthday party, a broken arm, or a disappointing Christmas. Maybe it was your parents' divorce, or a trip to Walt Disney World. When you visualize this experience, can you be sure of what you are remembering?

Perhaps you are remembering not the experience itself but someone else's repeated version of events. Maybe your family has always regaled everyone with this story. Maybe you yourself have repeated it to dozens of others. Maybe, for you, it's become such a part of your personal narrative that what you're really remembering is the remembering of the story, not the story itself. And, what is perhaps

most relevant to our modern age, maybe you're just remembering a picture of it.

A particularly interesting question for all of us, when it comes to *how* we remember what we remember, is what has become the norm in terms of documentation of our lives. Blogging, texting, posting to Facebook and Instagram, filling our phones with pictures—all these activities are creating digital narratives and records that go beyond the wildest dreams of people from even a generation ago. If, as Loftus has shown, our memories are particularly susceptible to being falsely influenced by others' suggestions, then won't we, more and more, be remembering not so much the major events of our lives as someone's digital retelling of them? The pictures that we are bombarded with on a daily basis now cover even the most mundane aspects of our lives. Experiences and events that would never have been deemed filmworthy a generation or two ago now clog our photo collections. And when we post those pictures on a blog or other online platform, we essentially add a new layer of distortion with respect to the original experience.

Loftus's work has shown us, without a doubt, that memory is subject to serious flaws, not just when it comes to mundane events or single moments but even when it comes to whether events have occurred at all. As our documentation of our lives increases exponentially, we might well wonder where we will even begin to find the real memories beneath it all.

Developmental Psychology

A baby is not just a miniature child, and a child is not just a miniature adult; spend any amount of time with either of them, and this becomes evident rather quickly. But how do babies actually turn into children, and children into adults? Are the cognitive processes of these different age groups qualitatively different or just on different places on the spectrum of advancement? What is a normal developmental pace for a child, and what does it take in the way of biological and environmental influences for a cooing, crying, pooping bundle to become a reasoning, emoting, walking, talking individual?

Developmental psychologists are interested in changes across the life span. They recognize, more than any other branch within psychology, that different ages have different characteristics, and they have set out to observe and quantify those different characteristics, formulating theories about their causes and effects. Sometimes the term *developmental psychology* is used synonymously with *child psychology*, but, as many theorists have argued, development is a process that doesn't end when adulthood begins. Developmental psychologists have set out to study the biological, cognitive, emotional, and interpersonal changes that unfold across our lives, with some changes reflecting universal patterns and others largely affected by culture. And they seek to find out what makes these different stages of development happen, illuminating various factors that help turn us into the people we become and telling us quite a lot about the seasons of life in the process.

Jean Piaget

BORN 1896, Neuchâtel, Switzerland

DIED 1980, Geneva, Switzerland

Educated at the University
of Neuchâtel and the University
of Zurich

BIG IDEA

Jean Piaget's name is known to virtually anyone who takes a scholarly interest in child development, from teachers to therapists to medical doctors. He referred to his area of work on the origins of knowledge as **genetic epistemology**. (Note that *genetic* in this sense does not refer to genes and biology but rather to how something emerges and develops.) Piaget's ideas were a departure from earlier theories of intellectual development, as he felt that intelligence grows qualitatively with age, not just quantitatively. And he insisted that it grows in an active way that depends on a child's interactions with his or her environment. The latter idea is often said to reflect a **constructivist** way of thinking.

Schemas, or schemata—the mental structures that we use to make sense of our experiences, and that help us organize our environment by allowing us to categorize our perceptions and knowledge into patterns—are an important building block of Piaget's work. (Piaget was the first to apply the term *schemas* in a systematic way to psychology, originally calling them *schemes*.) Schemas create shortcuts for us, though they can sometimes lead to stereotyping. A schema can be represented by anything from "Cars have four wheels," to "If I let go of a toy I'm holding, it will fall." Piaget suggested that there are different types of schemas that depend on one's stage of development. Babies, for example, can use only behavioral schemas; an object has meaning only if it is in front of a baby who is acting on it. Older children, on the other hand, can conduct cognitive operations with an object, developing schemas that involve more general rules as to its qualities.

Piaget proposed that, over time, children learn to adjust their schemas, not just through combining them but also through adapting them to their environments. This process of adaptation entails two complementary aspects: **assimilation** and **accommodation**. Assimilation is the attempt to fit the outside world into a schema that the child already has. Let's say a child has a schema for oranges, knowing that an orange is a round fruit. One day the child is faced with a mandarin orange. It is much smaller than what the child is used to, but it fits the child's existing schema, so the child now has a new type of orange there. The child is assimilating it into his schema. But let's say that one day he is faced with a grapefruit. It, too, looks basically like an orange, and so he considers it to be one. But let's say he tastes it, and—whoa! It is very different from the oranges he knows so well. He must therefore adapt his existing schema to take this new information into account. After hearing the explanation of a grapefruit, he now changes his current schema to encompass the fact that not all round fruits are oranges. This is accommodation. (The fact that grapefruit have

nothing in common with grapes will have to be tackled when the child is older.)

Piaget theorized that these processes are what create intellectual growth, and he recognized that cultural and environmental factors can speed up or slow down that growth. But he also argued that growth always unfolds in a particular order, and his best-known theory lays out four sequential stages of that development: the **sensorimotor, preoperational, concrete operational,** and **formal operational** stages.

During the *sensorimotor* stage, as its name implies, a baby is focused on decoding her environment through her senses and beginning to understand how her body can move within her environment. Piaget said this stage begins at birth and starts with the reflexes newborns are equipped with. According to Piaget, over the course of the next two years, an explosion of growth moves the child along from having only reflexes as a tool to actually being able to think about her environment much more critically. There are several substages and much action in these first two years. From the ages of 1 to 4 months, infants start to control their behaviors (for example, cooing and finding their thumbs to suck on). But they are still focused on their own bodies. By 8 months, they are more purposefully interacting with external objects, and by 12 months, they are becoming more intentional, and they're coordinated enough to lift, to grasp, and to chain behaviors together, moving toward true goal setting. By 18 months, a child will begin to experiment more with objects, learning just what happens when she throws her bowl of soup on the floor. And by 24 months, she is constructing mental images and beginning to think symbolically. She is developing true insight into how to solve problems (or perhaps create new ones for her parents: "If I move that chair up to the kitchen counter, I'll be able to climb up onto it!"). Throughout the sensorimotor stage, **object permanence** solidifies. That's the understanding that objects continue to exist even when the child can't immediately see or otherwise sense them. This isn't automatic knowledge upon birth (one reason peekaboo is so thrilling).

The *preoperational* stage, from about the age of 2 until the age of 7, sees an overwhelming increase in language and representational thought. Early in this period, symbolic play develops: tea parties without real tea, horses that are really broomsticks, and even the presence of imaginary friends. We also see animism at this stage—the attribution of living qualities to inanimate objects ("The clouds are sad, and that's why it's raining."). And Piaget argued that egocentrism is a defining characteristic in the early part of this stage, with the child assuming that others all share his point of view; there's an inability to draw the line between himself and others. A child exhibiting egocentrism assumed that because he saw his brother take an extra cookie, his mother also knows about the transgression, even if she wasn't in the room to witness it.

Also observed within the beginning of this stage is lack of understanding of the principle of **conservation of quantity**; a young preoperational child cannot tell that when juice from a tall, skinny glass is poured into a shorter, broader glass, it is still the same amount of juice.

Next is the *concrete operational* stage. Thought to typically last from about the age of 7 until the age of 11, it is the stage when children become able to solve problems with logic and various other mental strategies that are much more systematic than those they used in the previous stage. A child at this stage can understand the connection between related parts of a series—this is understanding of **transitivity**—and can mentally arrange items along a scale by degree, as when she mentally lines up her classmates by height (this is called **mental seriation**).

Finally, starting at about the age of 11 or 12 and continuing until the end of life, comes the *formal operational* stage. Now abstract thinking becomes possible, and philosophical ideas, hypotheses, and systematic solutions to larger problems take hold. Children and teenagers at this stage will show deductive reasoning—the ability to take general principles and apply them to specific cases. People at this stage can also start to question the world's structures in abstract ways; it's why a preteen is able to pick up on political hypocrisy.

Though some of the exact skills and abilities Piaget spelled out for each stage have been refined and challenged in the decades since, and though some

theories of intelligence have emerged that look at separate intelligences rather than at wholesale stages of development, Piaget's name is a blockbuster one because of the exhaustive data he collected and the attention he gave to understanding individual children's mental processes. He laid the foundation for understanding mental development from birth to adulthood, and his theories are still put to use in many settings.

THEN WHAT?

Decades of study within developmental psychology were directly spurred on by Jean Piaget's findings and by the new techniques he developed, including individual clinical interviews with children aimed at understanding their mental processes. Piaget's ideas about the necessity of active learning and the importance of meeting a child where he is developmentally, rather than trying desperately to speed him up to the next stage, still have many followers today.

WHAT ABOUT ME?

If you've ever tried to talk with a child at Piaget's concrete operational stage, you may have come face to face with just how concrete she can be—in fact, you may wonder how to handle this when it comes to explaining the world around her. Perhaps she has already internalized that smoking cigarettes is unhealthy or that honesty is the best policy. That is all great, of course, and yet when it comes to the messier nuances of the real world, her mindset may butt up against more complex realities. It can be downright impossible for a child at this stage to think in more abstract terms, and it can lead to some rather awkward situations: "Grandma must be dumb because she smokes," or "I need to tell the truth—Uncle Justin is getting fat."

On a lighter note, perhaps you've had the misfortune of scooping ice cream into bowls at a 4-year-old's birthday party. Maybe you gave one child two small scoops and the birthday boy one big one. Watch out! The birthday boy might just launch an all-out mutiny. If he is not yet able to understand the principle of conservation of quantity, he sees his one scoop as woefully inferior to the two scoops given to his buddy.

Another classic Piagetian concept is the **A-not-B error**, also called the *perseverative error*. Let's say you have two boxes (A and B), a toy, and a baby between the ages of 8 and 12 months. If you repeatedly show the baby that you are putting the toy in box A, she will learn to look for it in box A. But then you mix it up—let's say you show her that you've put the toy in box B. She will likely still look for it in box A because that is where she found it previously. Piaget believed that this error persists because of the baby's behavioral schema. The baby can't understand that the toy can be put somewhere that has nothing to do with where *she* last found it. Other arguments have since been developed as to why this error exists, but Piaget was the first to identify it.

We all know people who enjoy certain stages of childrearing more than others. Some people like the snuggly "baby burrito" stage, others the "philosophizing teenager" phase, and still others some stage in between. Have you ever really thought about why this is, however? It's likely not the child's ability to walk or drive, or how tall he is. It's who he is mentally. For every stage of a child's development, we have a classic snapshot in our heads of what makes that child tick; we fundamentally understand that a 3-year-old, a 6-year-old, a 9-year-old, and a 12-year-old will say and believe very different things. These mental differences are qualitative and meaningful; they're not just matters of degree. And Piaget was a pioneer in systematically measuring these differences and quantifying them for the world at large.

Lev Vygotsky

BORN 1896, Orsha, Russian Empire

DIED 1934, Moscow, Soviet Union

Educated at Moscow State University and at Shaniavskii Moscow City People's University

BIG IDEA

Lev Vygotsky was the rare psychological theorist whose ideas explode with popularity decades after his or her death. In Vygotsky's case, the delay was due in part to the slow pace of translation of some of his works, originally written in his native Russian. Some of them lay dormant for years before being introduced to Western theorists, and some were even censored for a while. The additional reason is that he died far too young; he had far too little time for his theories to be recognized before he succumbed to tuberculosis at the age of 37.

Vygotsky was one of the earliest psychological theorists to take culture meaningfully into account. His overall developmental theory is considered **sociocultural** in nature, and it involves two main theses. The first is that cognitive growth depends on the culture and social influences of one's environment. And the second is that learning itself is primarily social in nature, and that our cognitive capabilities grow more advanced through interactions with others more competent than we are.

Vygotsky viewed development itself as unfolding on four different levels, all of them interrelated:

» **Microgenetic** development is defined as small changes that occur over brief periods of time.

» **Ontogenetic** development occurs over the entire course of an individual's life (this is the type of development on which many developmental psychologists primarily focus).

» **Phylogenetic** development has to do with evolutionary forces that shape development over thousands of years.

» **Sociohistorical** development has to do with cultural changes that have made a difference in our experiences and in the ways we learn.

In an important departure from other theories of development, Vygotsky felt that culture matters so much that an individual's development depends on his or her culture, with people from different cultures not necessarily passing through the same stages cognitively or intellectually.

One of Vygotsky's best-known theories involves what he called the **zone of proximal development**. This zone is found in the gap between what a learner can do on her own and what she can do with the encouragement and guidance of someone more advanced. Vygotsky considered this the sweet spot, where real cognitive growth happens, and good teachers focus their efforts on this zone. Let's say a toddler is looking at her older brother's wooden train tracks. She tries to fit them together on her own but can't construct much; she puts two pegs together rather than matching up a peg with a hole. Her brother, though he sometimes shoos her away, is feeling kind, and he sits down on the floor with her and shows her how the matching pieces fit. She does this at first with his help, as he presses along with her to help her secure the pieces snugly together. Soon she can do it on her own, and before long she has constructed a track 2 feet long. Because her brother met her within the zone of proximal development, neither giving her directions way over her head nor replicating the mistakes she was making, she was able to learn, and her growth has taken off accordingly.

In Vygotsky's view, learning is more active and collaborative than it appears in the passive or self-directed processes postulated by other theories. Learning involves teachers who carefully tailor their lessons to the needs of their learners. Any teacher who believes in meeting students exactly where they are individually is operating within this theory, and if teachers do their work well, they will likely see successful student growth. And cooperation between the learner and the teacher, whether the teacher is a sibling, a friend, a parent, a coach, or an official school instructor, increases the learner's motivation and encourages the learner to work through problems and develop effective strategies for accomplishing tasks and mastering skills.

Vygotsky argued that different cultures have different **tools of intellectual adaptation**, which are the structures that a culture puts in place to help individuals learn. Different communities, in view of their needs, vary widely in the skills they prize. If you grew up in a place where you hunted for your food from a young age, you likely developed enhanced spatial skills relative to others your age living in other cultures. Or let's say you had artist parents who always focused a lot on teaching and appreciating different colors of the spectrum. In that case, it could very well be that your color-discrimination ability took off in early childhood and remains excellent.

Vygotsky posited that the process of development, helped by culture and interactive learning with others more skilled than we are, is how elementary mental functions grow into higher mental functions. Elementary mental functions are those that infants are born with, such the ability to sense things, attend to stimuli, perceive the world around them, and remember various experiences. Higher mental functions come in time, directly spurred on by the sociocultural experiences that make learning happen.

THEN WHAT?

Though some of his works took decades to be translated, Lev Vygotsky's popularity has not slowed down. His theories have been widely embraced within education, and they influenced other notable developmental psychologists, such as Jean Piaget. Vygotsky had a wide range of collaborators with whom he shared his ideas, and together they made up an informal group known as the Vygotsky Circle, whose theories about the social and cultural aspects of psychology spurred further study.

WHAT ABOUT ME?

Vygotsky's theories about cultural tools of intellectual adaptation seem to have been particularly ahead of their time, as contemporary research on a variety of skill sets gives us new examples of the ways his ideas apply across cultures

Number systems have gained particular attention lately. Different languages have different ways of naming numbers. In Japan, for example, which uses a base-10 naming system, as do China, Turkey, North Korea, and South Korea, there is a consistent and systematic way of naming numbers that includes the base-10 logic throughout, with the number 11 called the equivalent of "10-1," the number 12 called "10-2," and so on, whereas the naming conventions for numbers in English-speaking countries are idiosyncratic and don't follow the same consistent logic. One possible result, as cross-cultural research has suggested, is that American preschoolers show deficits in number fluency that may even continue through adulthood.

Another fascinating area of research, which began long after Vygotsky's time but nonetheless illuminates why his theories still have such value, concerns the notion of perfect or absolute pitch. Long a coveted trait among musicians, perfect pitch is the ability to identify the exact pitch of a musical note without having a reference point, a fun party trick whereby someone can accurately call out "C-sharp!" after a fork is clinked to a glass. Many of the most talented and disciplined musicians never possess this skill, whereas those who do have it often display it in early childhood, during musical training. It was long thought to be a genetic fluke. But recent research shows that it may be more environmentally derived than previously realized and may illustrate Vygotsky's concept of tools of adaptation. There is a higher prevalence of perfect pitch in places where the spoken language is a tonal language. In a tonal language, such as Mandarin or Cantonese, listeners must learn to distinguish tonal fluctuations between words that otherwise would sound the same, because these differences in tone, or pitch, give the words different meanings. For example, the sound *ma*, when pronounced as if being read aloud, connotes scolding. Pronounced as a ques-tion—*ma?*—it has the meaning of "rough." And *ma-a-a*, drawn out in a whine, means "horse." (This sound can indeed mean "mother" as well, if it's pronounced at a higher starting pitch.) But in English,

there are no such differences. Sure, tone and pitch can convey a lot about your emotional state or about which words of a sentence you want to emphasize, or about whether something is a question or a statement. But individual words don't become different words simply because of what tone they are on the scale. If you say *elbow* in a high pitch or a low pitch, it has the same meaning. If you say *el* high and *bow* low, or *el* low and *bow* high, it simply doesn't matter—it's known and understood as the same word. Vygotsky's theory would suggest that because speakers of tonal languages are forced to learn to pay attention to, and eventually discriminate among, these tones from the time they first begin to hear people speak, they are more likely to develop perfect pitch. Vygotsky never investigated this issue himself, but his theories were prescient, and they show that it is not just our genetics or our individual expe-riences but also the tools of our cultures that explain how we become who we are.

Harry Harlow

—●———●—

BORN 1905, Fairfield, Iowa

DIED 1981, Tucson, Arizona

Educated at Reed College and
Stanford University

BIG IDEA

Many people are familiar with Harry Harlow's classic study of rhesus monkeys raised without their mothers from infancy. In this study, he pitted surrogate mothers made of wire and wood against surrogate mothers made of terry cloth to see which surrogates the monkeys preferred (only the wire-and-wood surrogates provided milk). Less known, however, is the scope of Harlow's research, which included a number of other monkey studies that went beyond comparing terry-cloth surrogates to wood-and-wire surrogates. Indeed, Harlow's extensive work was instrumental in propelling forward big ideas about attachment and peer relationships.

In Harlow's most noteworthy study, monkeys craved the contact comfort of terry cloth more than they valued the ability to be nourished by milk. Of course, it makes sense that it was more comfortable for them to sit on terry cloth than on wire and wood. But the level to which the monkeys gravitated toward the terry-cloth surrogates, especially in times of fear, spoke to something larger about attachment. We see this in human children, who are comforted by stuffed animals or other cuddly toys. Harlow's discovery went squarely against the psychoanalytic **cupboard model** of previous theories on mother-child attachment, which had said that the mother provides nourishment

KEY EXPERIMENT Harry Harlow used rhesus monkeys for his experiments, and his most classic experiment looked at monkeys who had been raised from infancy without their mothers. He had two different cages for each monkey, and each cage contained a primitive mother figure, or surrogate. One of the surrogates was made of wire and wood, and the other was covered in terry cloth. Even though only the wire-and-wood surrogate had a nipple that yielded milk, the monkeys overwhelmingly preferred to spend time with their terry-cloth surrogates. When the monkeys were frightened, they tended to cling to their terry-cloth surrogates and never once went to the milk-yielding surrogates when they were afraid.

Harlow also observed monkeys that were raised in isolation for anywhere from three months to one year. Three months of isolation had minimal effects, but longer periods of isolation were striking for the damage they seemed to cause. When finally faced with other monkeys, the previously isolated monkeys tended to sit in a corner rocking, sometimes biting themselves; they showed no interest or ability in playing and were unable to fight back if provoked. Later, when some of these monkeys became parents themselves, they tended to ignore or even attack their offspring. This behavior in the adult monkeys was most pronounced toward their firstborn offspring, but the experience of parenthood seemed to teach the previously isolated monkeys better ways to behave, and they behaved in less problematic ways with subsequent offspring.

and satisfies basic biological needs, and that therein lies the origin of the bond with her child. Harlow's findings also went against the behaviorist model, which said that children are conditioned to be attached to their mothers because of the positive reinforcement and conditioning of having their biological needs met. In addition, his findings helped dislodge the prevailing mindset of the time, which held that too much physical cuddling and comforting can spoil a baby. Furthermore, the presence of the surrogates allowed the monkeys to be more adventurous. They took more healthy risks in venturing out when their surrogates were near, showing how a strong attachment that provides comfort can help lay the foundation of security that provides the confidence to be more autonomous in the world.

Harlow's findings also suggest how strongly we attach to the faces of those we love. The terry-cloth surrogates were given slightly different faces, and each monkey not only came to know and recognize its own surrogate's face but also clearly preferred its surrogate over others that were similar.

What gets less attention is Harlow's exploration of the role of peers, in terms of attachment and development. In one aspect of his experimentation, Harlow compared monkeys who had contact only with their mothers to monkeys who had contact only with their peers. Neither group fared particularly well. The monkeys who were in the mother-only contact group failed to develop healthy social behaviors when finally exposed to their peers, they would avoid them or even become highly aggressive. The monkeys in the peer-only contract group would cling to the peers they had grown to know but were aggressive toward monkeys outside the peer group when finally exposed to them. In general, they were more irritable and agitated than the monkeys in the mother-only contact group.

Harlow's most heartening research involved the addition of carefully screened monkey "therapists." The monkeys serving in the therapeutic role would hang around with the previously isolated monkeys, clinging to them. In time, the previously isolated monkeys clung back, and their behavior began to look more normal and adaptive, in terms of their interactions with others, though it's worth noting that they always remained more acutely susceptible to stress.

Harlow felt strongly that he was revealing deeper truths that apply to the human experience. Strikingly, he said that the focus of his studies was love, not attachment, even though many theorists overwhelmingly preferred the latter focus. Harlow himself, however, was unsentimental, and he openly acknowledged that he didn't really like animals and had no love for the monkeys he had spent years experimenting on. Some people consider his experiments to have been unethical by their very nature.

THEN WHAT?

Harlow's work on monkey attachment directly influenced later researchers on human attachment, including his students John Bowlby and Mary Ainsworth, later famed for their exploration of different attachment styles. For example, Ainsworth developed the "strange situation" task, which has been used for decades to study the strength of young children's attachments to their parents or caregivers and to observe their responses in somewhat stressful situations. Children between the age of 12 months and 24 months are the typical participants. In this experimental setup, a stranger is introduced to each child in the presence of his or her caregiver, and then the caregiver leaves the child alone with the stranger. Later the caregiver comes back and the stranger leaves, and then the caregiver leaves again and the stranger returns. Finally, the children are reunited with their caregivers. The various steps of this process are observed by researchers

through two-way mirrors, with specific attention given to the children's emotional responses, their ability to soothe themselves and play, and their ability to be soothed by the strangers and/or by their own caregivers. Ainsworth categorized the patterns she observed into those that reflected *secure attachment* and those that reflected *insecure attachment*, with the latter set further categorized as reflecting an *insecure-avoidant* pattern of attachment (the children showed few emotional reactions and little connection to their caregivers) and an *insecure-resistant* pattern of attachment (the children were so distressed by the departure and even

the return of their caregivers that it was difficult for them to be consoled). Later, a colleague of Ainsworth's, Mary Main, added the category of a *disorganized/ disoriented* pattern of attachment, which included mixed distress signals and disorientation upon a caregiver's return. With this work, Ainsworth helped establish attachment theory, which posits that the strength of young children's attachments to primary caregivers helps set the stage for many aspects of later development. The specific attachment styles she identified have been shown to have implications for later personality traits, emotional health, and interpersonal relationships.

WHAT ABOUT ME?

Whether you've spent one afternoon or 10 straight years with babies, you've probably picked up on the fact that they like to be held. Close contact, warmth, and proximity soothe them in an immediately noticeable way. In fact, holding a baby can often be the only thing that will stop his or her crying, much to the frustration of a parent who hasn't slept well in weeks.

New parents are often bombarded with messages about the right way to do things, and many birth mothers feel shamed and anxious if they are unable to breast-feed their babies, believing that the mother-infant bond may be in jeopardy. But it's the cuddling and comfort of feeding, not the exact mechanism of the milk's delivery, that clearly makes for good bonding. Thankfully, this provides a chance for others besides a biological mother to bond beautifully as well, whether feeding the baby bottled breast milk or formula.

Harlow's studies on monkeys raised without any parenting at all also force us to think in stark ways about how the quality of our early attachments can influence our later attachments. Harlow's findings suggest that if we are not shown love ourselves, it will be difficult for us to know how to show it to others. Perhaps your parents were the opposite of affectionate, and their coldness and sternness translated into rejection. Or perhaps there was even abuse. Your experiences of trying to find love in young adulthood might have

left you feeling completely out of sorts, not knowing what it means to express affection, how to go about it, how far you should go to do it, or what it should feel like. Maybe you overcompensated and jumped into a whirlwind relationship with the first person who ever complimented you. Or maybe someone treated you well, and you cared for that person a great deal, but his or her nurturing was so foreign to you that it made you uncomfortable. It's not uncommon for people who have never been shown much open affection to have no idea how to act when it's finally shown to them, and they may become profoundly doubtful and ill at ease.

The same feelings might apply if you did not have parents who were particularly loving but eventually go on to have your own children. Perhaps you feel you have no "script" for how to show affection to your kids: "Is my praise too much?" "I feel self-conscious cooing back at my baby." "Do people actually say *I love you* to their kids at bedtime?" "Do I hug my kids at preschool pickup?" You love your children a great deal, and you wish that expressing it came naturally, but it just doesn't seem to. Harlow's studies show that this is less likely to be a problem with your genes than a challenge you must overcome because of the deficits in your early attachments.

But the good news is that the challenge can be overcome. Just like Harry Harlow's monkey "therapists," other people in your life can make a difference with their encouraging, patient, empathetic support. These people may be the surrogate families you developed among your high school friends' parents, a first real confidant, neighbors or colleagues, a romantic partner, or a psychotherapist. Past deficits can be undone. Lack of warmth and comfort in childhood may have played a part in the person that you've become, but that doesn't have to be the whole story.

Erik Erikson

BORN 1902, Frankfurt, Germany

DIED 1994, Cape Cod, Massachusetts

Educated at the Vienna
Psychoanalytic Institute

BIG IDEA

When you think of psychological development, you might very well think of young children growing into their personalities, or of kids in middle school gaining maturity. Perhaps you even think of finding yourself in your late teen years or in early college. Not as many of us will think of development as a lifelong process, though, one that continues long after our bodies have matured and our cognitive capacities are at their peak. Erik Erikson, however, taught the psychology field to view development as a process that continues until the day we take our last breath.

Erikson did not see developmental stages as tied to specific ages across the board for everyone. Rather, he believed that they are emotional and cognitive transitions whose emergence is dictated both by biological maturation and by the social demands that act on a person at any given point in life. Erikson's theory includes eight psychosocial stages, which, he postulated, all people go through, in consecutive order, throughout the life span. Each stage involves a basic conflict between two extremes; these are **life crises** that need to be sorted out. According to Erikson, successful navigation of the conflict results in the development of a certain virtue and paves the way for the next stage:

» The first stage, in infancy, involves the conflict of *basic trust versus mistrust*, leading to the development of the virtue of hope, if successfully navigated. Babies must quickly learn to trust others and discern who will be responsible for meeting their needs. The primary caregivers serve as the key social agents at this stage, and if their caregiving is erratic or neglectful, the baby may come to view the world as a scary place that is unpredictable and perhaps even hopeless.

» Toddlerhood brings the conflict of *autonomy versus shame and doubt*, and if this crisis is resolved, it will lead to will. Toddlers are beginning to learn how to handle some parts of taking care of themselves, from using a spoon to using the toilet to falling asleep on their own. Parents are still the key social agents here, and if toddlers have difficulty establishing their independence, they will experience doubt and shame about their ability to navigate the world.

» The preschool years bring the conflict of *initiative versus guilt*, with successful navigation of this struggle leading to purpose. Children at this stage will sometimes bite off more than they can chew, in terms of the goals or activities that they attempt. This can create conflict with rules and other people and can sometimes cause guilt and being in trouble. But it can also engender children's growing confidence in what they can accomplish on their own. The family is the key social agent here.

» The grade school years, up to about the age of 12, bring the conflict of *industry versus inferiority*, with successful navigation leading to competence. This is when social comparisons between children and their peers start to become quite important, as children see themselves and their accomplishments in relation to others. If they are industrious and begin to master various academic and social skills, kids can feel self-assured by their successes. Otherwise, feelings of inferiority set in. Teachers and peers enter the scene here as significant social agents.

» From the teenage years to about the age of 20, there is the conflict of *identity versus role confusion*, with successful navigation leading to fidelity. Here lies the tension between being a child and being an adult, the essential but sometimes tumultuous push-pull of becoming a grown-up: "Who am I, really? What is my path in life, and what place do I have among people I care about?" This challenge can also be known as an **identity crisis**, a term first used by Erickson. The key social agents here, for better or for worse, are peers as teenagers try to establish their identities. But Erickson argued that supportive parents have a role in letting teenagers explore, without burdening them with excessively rigid expectations about who they should become.

» Erikson said that the next stage, typically associated with the early 20s until about the age of 40, involves the conflict of *intimacy versus isolation*, with successful resolution leading to love. This stage often brings an in-depth exploration of the nuances of real love and companionship, in both friendships and romantic relationships. Feeling a lack of true intimacy with others can bring loneliness.

» With middle adulthood comes the conflict of *generativity versus stagnation*, with successful navigation leading to care. What does productivity mean at work, in the family, and in life goals? Some people assume responsibility naturally; others resist, and stagnation follows. Cultural norms play a role as a key social agent here, as every culture decides for itself what it looks like to be generative. Spouses and children, when they are present, are also key social agents.

» Finally, older age brings the conflict of *ego integrity versus despair*, leading, if successfully navigated, to wisdom. In the late 60s and later, the individual begins to look back at his or her life and interpret its meaning. Ego integrity is the overall acceptance of one's life, with its highs as well as its lows. But a feeling of significant disappointment, with goals unrealized or expectations unmet, can lead to despair. And thus the key agent is no longer a current social one but rather the individual's interpretations and

memories of his or her own past social experiences. Successful navigation of this phase leads to wisdom and to the ability to find meaning and eventually accept one's life in the face of death.

Together, Erikson's psychosocial stages paint the full picture of a life. They emphasize our relationships with others and our changing emotions, from birth to old age, and they set his theory apart from previous developmental ones. Erikson also argued that our successful or unsuccessful navigation of these phases will create the triumphs and bruises that come to define our personalities.

THEN WHAT?

Erikson's theories led to a broadened view of what psychological development means, and they served as a bridge between psychoanalytic theory and a life-span model of development. That life-span model has led to greater interest in studies of aging and gerontology. Erikson also pioneered the biographical genre known as **psychohistory**; his historical/psychoanalytic study of Gandhi won Erikson a Pulitzer Prize.

WHAT ABOUT ME?

Whether you are 17, 43, or 91, take a moment to visualize some earlier stage of your development. There is a chance that your most vivid memories involve meeting biological milestones, or the ways in which you interacted with your physical environment. But you're most likely to see other people in your mind's eye. In fact, your memories of siblings, neighbors, friends, romantic partners, parents, colleagues, and teachers probably define the life stages for you, in ways that may be pleasant or not so pleasant.

Let's take middle childhood, Erikson's "industry versus inferiority" phase. You may not remember what all the cognitive milestones were for that stage, but you probably remember who was always beating you on spelling tests, who could shoot more baskets than you could, and whose popularity left you feeling shy and gangly. You may also remember how you first learned that you were good at art or could make your friends laugh. The indelible meanings of such early comparisons, which also lead us to start believing certain things about ourselves, stay with us for a very long time.

If you look back at yourself as an adolescent or a young adult, you'll see that the pattern continues. It is hard to forget your first crush, your first roommate, and the first boss who made you believe that you really did know what you were doing. The social aspects of life often seem to eclipse other influences in recollections of these years, especially when it comes

to reflecting on what your life has meant. Erikson's theory captures this reality in a remarkable way, showing that how we relate to others, and the needs we have for other people in terms of our own development, may vary with our life stages but never diminish in importance.

If you have always set goals for yourself, whether with checklists or with five-year plans, you may very well look back at your past goals and find them aligned with Erikson's eight psychosocial stages. From finding a spouse to launching a career to planning for retirement and making a bucket list, what is important during any given decade often follows a rather universal pattern. And though your particular culture may have imposed its own particular expectations (Was it assumed that you would go to college? Was it considered best to live off the land? Was it your responsibility above all else to raise your children?), there is little variance between cultures in the ways we relate to ourselves and find meaning in our relationships. From teenage angst to a midlife crisis, from redefining ourselves after retirement to determining how we want to live in our last years, we see Erikson's social and emotional stages over and over again.

Noam Chomsky

BORN 1928, Philadelphia, Pennsylvania

Educated at the University of Pennsylvania

BIG IDEA

There is no bigger contributor to theory at the intersection of linguistics and psychology than Noam Chomsky, though he is not a trained psychologist but rather a theorist with a Ph.D. in philosophy. And though a discussion of his work might fit well into other chapters of this book, his theories about the development of language make that discussion appropriate here, in this chapter about developmental psychology. Chomsky's theories are organized around his concept of **transformational grammar**, which has to do with the patterns and rules that a language uses, and with how new sentences can be formulated from existing sentences. Chomsky also continues to be a force as a political activist, an economic theorist, and a social critic.

From early on, Chomsky's work looked at the development of language, and he attacked the fundamental aspects of behaviorism as they pertained to language learning. In so doing, Chomsky became an important figure within the rising field of cognitive psychology. Recall that most behaviorists theorized that language is learned the way any other type of behavior is learned, through conditioning and repetition. Chomsky thinks this conception falls short of the truth. He believes that we are born pre-programmed to learn language, and that language learning is a process distinct and qualitatively different from the types of learning that go on in connection with other behaviors. Humans, Chomsky says, come with a built-in **language acquisition device (LAD)**, which exists in the brain and is qualitatively distinct and unique. This idea is considered to reflect a **nativist theory of language acquisition**, a theory that says we're genetically ingrained with the distinct ability to learn language. Chomsky sees the LAD as a processor that is set in motion by verbal input. He theorizes that the LAD entails inherent understanding of the structure of universal grammar, and that it gives children the ability to put words together in meaningful ways after they have learned some initial vocabulary.

Chomsky has made the case for this theory with his **poverty-of-stimulus** argument, which proposes that mere exposure to the stimulus of hearing people say particular sentences could never be sufficient to account for the ability of toddlers to learn how to speak. He argues that languages are so elaborate and complex that they can't possibly be taught only by parents and peers, or discovered through trial and error. There are innumerable basic, comprehensible sentences that have likely never been spoken before, Chomsky says, and yet we are already completely capable of both uttering and understanding them. If we were to hear them, we would understand them automatically and intuitively. Chomsky's critique of conditioning as the sole explanation for language development

is quite significant, and it hastened behaviorism's fall from dominance.

Chomsky has done a lot of work in the area of **syntax**, which has to do with the patterns of word arrangement that lead to meaning within phrases and sentences. He posits that any sentence has both a **deep structure** and a **surface structure.** The surface structure is in the way the words look and sound, whereas the deep structure has to do with the underlying meaning and allows for analysis and interpretation. The sentences "I love my parents." and "My parents are loved by me." have basically the same deep structure; they mean the same thing. Their surface structure, however, is different; the two sentences look different on the page and sound different to our ears. Chomsky has also explained that we derive meaning from **morphemes** and **phonemes**. *Morphemes* are the smallest bits of a language that still have some sort of meaning. In English, we have plenty of these nonwords that nonetheless are understood quite well, such as *ing* or *anti* or *un* or *ness*. Of course, plenty of actual words are themselves morphemes: *dog, top, snap*. Combine two or more morphemes into something new, and we understand what it means, whether it's a word (*unsnap, topless*) or not (*undog*). *Phonemes* are even smaller linguistic units; they are sounds (or gestures, in sign languages) that are recognized as belonging to a particular language and as being distinct from one another. American English has 26 letters but about

44 phonemes (perhaps the precise number depends on one's accent), as various letters can be used for different sounds (the long *o* in *open* and the short *o* in *on*), and letters can be combined to form whole new sounds (*ch* or *sh* or *th*). Though Chomsky is not the first theorist to talk about phonemes and morphemes, he has moved research significantly forward in this area and helped establish linguistics as a science. He has also embraced the linguist and neurologist Eric Lenneberg's theory of **critical periods of development** when it comes to language learning. This theory says that, just as in several aspects of biological growth, there is a window of time early in life when language learning must begin; if language learning doesn't begin during that time, then language will be markedly difficult to learn later on. The case of the pseudonymous Genie, a so-called feral child who was rescued at the age of 13 after years of severe neglect, isolation, and lack of stimulation, is often cited as evidence for this theory. Despite many interventions, Genie failed to become fluent in any spoken language, a result attributed to her having completely missed exposure to language input during that critical period.

Incidentally, Chomsky has stated that only humans come equipped with the LAD.

The fact that apes (including a chimpanzee pointedly named Nim Chimpsky) have been taught to use sign language shows that this is not necessarily the case. However, the question of whether animals can use language spontaneously or have rule-bound structures of grammar remains a matter of some controversy.

THEN WHAT?

Chomsky's influence on cognitive psychology, language development, and linguistics cannot be overstated. His critiques of behaviorism contributed to its demise as a full-spectrum explanation of behavior. His nativist understanding of language development has spurred decades of research into the nature of language acquisition in children, and his study of syntactical structures has pushed forward the study of cognitive science in general.

WHAT ABOUT ME?

A famed example of the difference between deep structure and surface structure involves this sentence: "The French bottle smells." Are we talking about how the French make perfume, or about a French bottle that is taking on a nasty odor? It depends on how we create the phrasing in our minds—what we make of its syntax. We can understand the words "The French bottle" as the subject of the sentence, or we can understand "The French" as the subject and "bottle" as a verb. Or consider the function served by a comma. There's a big difference between "I like cooking, my family, and my pets" and "I like cooking my family and my pets." As punctuation continues to go by the board with the explosion of texting as a form of communication, it will be interesting and often amusing to see the miscommunications that arise from the difference between surface structure and deep structure.

Carol Dweck

●━━●

BORN 1946, Brooklyn, New York

Educated at Columbia University
and Yale University

BIG IDEA

Of all the theorists discussed in this book, Carol Dweck is likely the most contemporary; her career is as active as can be. Dweck is best known for her implicit theories of intelligence, which explore where we believe our abilities come from. Like the work of Noam Chomsky, Dweck's work could have been discussed in several other chapters of this book, but that discussion is most appropriate in this chapter, given Dweck's research into raising and teaching children.

The research question that came to define Dweck's work is relatively simple:

Why do some children persist on a task after setbacks or failures, whereas other children give up or avoid attempting to perform the task in the first place? In 1978, Dweck observed that teachers and parents can inadvertently foster a sense of helplessness in a child when they blame the child's failure on lack of ability rather than on lack of effort. In other words, teachers who do this tend to ratify the child's conclusion, after she has done poorly on a math test, that she just isn't good at math, even if the actual problem is that she didn't practice enough or didn't spend enough time checking for careless mistakes. The child who thinks she's just poor at math will go on to question the value of making much of an effort at all, but if she believed that she could develop strategies for working harder and not making the same mistakes, she would be more motivated to try those strategies out in preparation for her next math test.

In her later research, Dweck began to look at how children are praised. As parents and teachers, we can praise traits and abilities ("What a great artist you are! You are so talented!") or we can praise effort ("Look at how carefully you drew that picture! You spent so much time on it, with all the different colors!"). Dweck discovered that the nature of the praise children receive is associated with how they tend to think of themselves, and specifically with what they think is responsible for their successes. Dweck was struck by the extent to which these associations come to affect not just how hard children are willing to try but also how afraid they are of failure, and how readily they bounce back from failure if it does occur.

Dweck's work has contrasted two different *mindsets* associated with the long-term use of different types of praise. Children who are constantly praised for their inherent abilities and traits will be more prone to develop the **fixed mindset**. These children think of their intelligence or abilities as static, unchangeable attributes. They think they're either smart or not smart, good at spelling or not good at spelling. If a child's self-assessment is poor—if the child believes that he is just never going to be intelligent—then it is clear how helpless he may feel, and how unmotivated he may become after a setback. But even if the child's self-assessment is good, Dweck has argued, his fixed mindset

will present serious drawbacks. A child who believes that everyone views him as smart will be more fearful of failure because he is desperate to keep proving everyone right. He doesn't want to make mistakes, lest he lose the "smart" mantle he's been wearing for so long. Terrified to do anything that might disprove the trait everyone says he possesses, he sticks to the tasks he's most comfortable with, the ones he already knows he can do well.

On the other hand, children with the **growth mindset** fare much better. This mindset, according to Dweck, is defined by the belief that effort and work will pay off, that one always has the potential to grow and get better at something, and that intelligence can be developed. The child with this mindset knows she is capable of trying hard, and she connects this knowledge with the idea that she can eventually overcome challenges. She is much less fearful of failure because she isn't bound by the belief that failure will automatically discount who she purports to be. Failure, instead of representing a wrecking ball aimed at the very core of her identity, simply indicates the need to practice longer, learn more, or come up with new strategies. She isn't crushed by setbacks, and so she is much less likely to shy away from challenges and much more likely to try things outside her comfort zone, bouncing back when she doesn't get the top score on a test.

Children's ability to view their abilities as malleable may have implications for areas beyond how much effort they put into a math test or how willing they are to try a new sport. As a culture, we tend to have beliefs about who is good at what, and it is thought that these beliefs may even affect who chooses to go into what fields. Women's underrepresentation in science and engineering, for example, may have something to do with the messages that girls pick up about what girls are naturally supposed to be capable of. As children grow, and as school and life in general become more challenging, especially during the emotional upheaval of the teen years, their mindsets may determine which of them will continue to achieve and even improve (those will be the kids with the growth mindset) and which of them will see their academic performance decline (the kids with the fixed mindset).

The question of whether one has the fixed or the growth mindset continues to be relevant in adulthood. For better or for worse, and long after our school days have ended, many of us continue to recognize in ourselves one of these mindsets, and its effects, when it comes to how we see our intelligence and abilities. Thankfully, the growth mindset can be built and learned.

THEN WHAT?

Dweck's research is still in the process of revolutionizing many different facets of education and performance. Her ideas have become absorbed into school systems and educational curricula and have made their way into mainstream parenting advice. Athletic coaches and music teachers have also been widely affected by her findings, which have spurred additional research into motivation, performance, and the internalization of praise.

WHAT ABOUT ME?

If you are a parent, you may already be familiar with some of Dweck's research. Perhaps you've observed other parents praising their children's efforts rather than their abilities. Nevertheless, whenever a psychological theory is adopted by large numbers of people who are not psychologists, something may get lost in translation. Dweck has expressed concern that, as effort is praised more and more (a good thing in general), effort itself may become the main focus, at the expense of the finer nuances of the growth mindset. In Dweck's theory, effort is not meant to be the main goal but rather a means to achieve learning. Empty praise for effort that doesn't result in any new learning ("Great try! Your paper airplane doesn't fly, but you gave it your all!") may not do much good, in contrast with praise for effort that focuses on learning new ways to overcome challenges. ("Great try! You really put a lot into it. I wonder what you could do differently next time to get it to fly farther.") In other words, simply telling a child to do his best and then giving him a gold star for effort can backfire if the effort doesn't lead anywhere, as it's not really creating new insights within the child, and it may even subtly teach him to adopt a fixed mindset about the likelihood that he'll continue to fail.

There is also some concern that as Dweck's theories grow more and more prevalent in American education systems—her 2006 book *Mindset: The New Psychology of Success* continues to be quite popular—the notion of the growth mindset itself may become little more than a meaningless buzzword if it is not correctly understood. For example, many teachers know that they are supposed to embody the growth mindset, and that they should even use the term *growth mindset* to demonstrate their familiarity with up-to-date educational theory. But the problem is that the popularity of Dweck's ideas may lead to the creation of *false* growth mindsets if the fixed mindset is understood only as something to be feared and covered up. It may also be too easily forgotten that nurturing the growth mindset is not just about praising children's successes but also about helping kids bounce back from failure. Dweck's

more recent research has identified some teaching patterns that espouse the growth mindset but still react to mistakes as harmful and to be avoided. In reality, for Dweck, failure is a way to learn.

Perhaps you think that Dweck's theories sound a bit too much like "All of you are super smart!" and that they reek of the "Trophies for everyone!" parenting practices that appeared during the 1980s. Such practices, said to result from a misguided focus on the importance of self-esteem, still seem prevalent in many quarters. But Dweck's theory actually runs completely counter to those practices. It focuses not on covering up differences in ability and pretending that everyone is the same but on meeting children individually where they are and helping them do their best. The truest applications of Dweck's theory don't use indiscriminate or meaningless praise. Instead, they demonstrate that effort brings learning, and that learning—even and perhaps especially the kind of learning that comes through mistakes—brings improvement.

Psychology of Personality

Personality: it's why we hate some people and love others. It's what makes us act differently from our friends and family and coworkers, and it's what accounts for our essence as individuals, distinct from those around us. Personality is defined as the set of enduring psychological characteristics that differentiate us from each other, and these characteristics result in behavior patterns that tend to be predictable across situations. How do you know your mom is going to be upset when the waiter gets her order wrong? It's a matter of personality. She'll act differently from your dad or your sister or your boss because the latter people are walking around with different sets of traits altogether.

Personality psychologists believe that individual differences are most salient in explaining behavior. They acknowledge that certain general rules may govern human nature, but that the specific traits we walk around with—from a sarcastic tongue to a fondness for order, from a fear of conflict to a tendency to talk someone's ear off—will matter most of all. Of all the areas of study within psychology, it is the psychology of personality that most focuses on what makes us distinct, in good ways and in bad. And the field has spent decades seeking to understand how the specific traits that make up our personalities can be quantified and understood, work that has led to theories that go a long way toward explaining why we do the things we do.

Gordon Allport

—•—

BORN 1897, Montezuma, Indiana

DIED 1967, Cambridge, Massachusetts

Educated at Harvard University and Cambridge University

BIG IDEA

Considered one of the early founders of personality psychology, Gordon Allport rejected psychoanalysis. He felt it went so deep as to go off on meaningless tangents, latching on to red herrings as an explanation of behavior. And behaviorism, Allport argued, did not go nearly deep enough. Allport developed theories that allowed for the interaction of personality traits and behavior, examining how individual differences play out in one's environment. And

his beliefs about the purpose of the self crossed over into humanistic psychology, a field in which he also can be seen to have exerted considerable influence.

One famous and entertaining anecdote that exemplifies Allport's frustration with psychoanalysis involves his 1922 meeting with the founder of psychoanalysis, Sigmund Freud. Allport was in his early 20s at the time and had taken a train to Vienna for the conversation. Upon Allport's arrival, Freud was silent. Attempting to break the ice, Allport described a situation he had witnessed on the train: A young boy, who clearly was highly bothered by dirt, objected to sitting in places where dirty people had sat or next to strangers whom he viewed as unclean. Allport suggested to Freud that the boy's mother, who had seemed rather domineering, might have played a role in the development of this attitude. After Allport completed this story, Freud looked at him and asked, "And was that little boy you?"

It almost reads like a joke—Freud being so Freudian as to almost be a caricature. But to Allport, this awkward exchange exemplified what he viewed as the problems of psychoanalysis. No, the boy was not him; and, no, he wouldn't have told the story in such a way if the boy had been him. Surely, he thought, psychoanalytic explanations of behavior are not always accurate and are sometimes on the wrong path entirely.

Allport was an early proponent of trait theories. Traits are specific characteristics within our personalities that not only differentiate us from each other but also stay constant over time. According to Allport, not only do we possess different types of traits, they also exist at different levels of significance within us. **Cardinal traits** are the rarest, and they are so central to an individual's personality that they pretty much define it. Not everyone has these; only certain people do (for example, Ebenezer Scrooge, whose very existence is synonymous with the trait of stinginess). **Central traits** are not all-encompassing but work together to form our personalities; we each tend to have five to ten of these. They include things like honesty and aggressiveness. And **secondary traits** are present only in certain circumstances; they include preferences and attitudes that can be more specific than the more general types of traits. Perhaps you are extremely anxious at very large parties or

become very irritable when rushed. The notion of secondary traits allows for the importance of situational factors, a consideration that many other trait theories do not account for. The baggage of the word *trait* eventually became so significant, in terms of its connotations of strict, quantifiable definitions, that Allport changed it to *disposition*, which allows for different manifestations of a particular characteristic in different situations and among different people. Curiosity, for example, does not necessarily look the same in two different people. Allport also recognized that traits common in one culture are not necessarily common in another.

Allport's term for the self is **proprium**, which emphasizes the qualities that move us forward and propel us toward growth. He theorized that some personality traits are more tied to our proprium than others are. Naturally, if you possess cardinal traits, they define you far more than secondary traits do, and central traits fall somewhere in the middle. Allport used the term *propriate functioning* to refer to things that we do because they align with our true selves, with the way we view ourselves, and with our role within the world.

He coined the term *functional autonomy* to refer to our ability to act fully in the present; the origins of our motives don't matter nearly as much as the motives themselves. Allport didn't believe (as the psychoanalysts did) that we have to be tied to the burdens of the past. According to Allport, at any moment we are capable of acting with conscious free will and are not overwhelmingly driven by the unconscious. But **perseverative functional autonomy** allows for the idea that certain behaviors can persist just by force of habit, long after their initial purpose has been served. For example, let's say that in your early 20s you lived in an incredibly noisy apartment complex, and so you used a white-noise machine so you could fall asleep at night. You did this for years. Now you are in your 50s and have long since lived in quiet places, but you still use the white-noise machine. At some point, you got so used to it that now you can barely sleep without it, even though its original purpose no longer applies and it's no longer needed to actually reduce background noise.

Propriate functional autonomy is less the result of habits than of values. It has to do with behaving in ways that reflect who we believed ourselves to be. Allport, along with his colleagues Philip Vernon and Gardner Lindzey, developed a measure of values that was in use for several decades. It was based on six types of values identified in 1914 by the German psychologist Eduard Spranger: theoretical, economic, aesthetic, social, political, and religious.

Finally, moving more toward what aligns well with humanistic psychology, Allport had ideas about what it means to reach psychological maturity. He theorized that such maturity occurs as a combination of having an adaptable and healthy set of traits and having a well-developed proprium (that is, the sense of self aligned with those traits). The attainment of maturity comes about on the basis of seven different criteria, all of them ways of relating to the world:

» Extensions of the self, which mean involvement with others and the community
» Warm relating, which refers to trust, genuineness, and empathy for others
» Emotional security and the ability to accept oneself
» Realistic perception, which allows one to be honest about oneself rather than defensive
» Problem-centeredness, which allows one to overcome challenges
» Self-objectification, which lets one really know oneself and see the big picture
» A philosophy of life that is cohesive and includes a conscience that one has developed to be true to oneself

THEN WHAT?

Gordon Allport's theories not only influenced later personality researchers but also had an impact on the humanistic therapies of Abraham Maslow and Carl Rogers. Allport's noteworthy students include Stanley Milgram and Anthony Greenwald, whose Implicit Association Test (developed with Mahzarin Banaji) broke new ground in how we think about bias and showed just how prevalent various unconscious biases are among wide ranges of people.

WHAT ABOUT ME?

How do you define yourself? Are you kind sometimes? Rarely? Almost always? Maybe you're just average on the kindness scale, the same as millions of others. In that case, kindness does not seem to define you one way or another. It's not a cardinal trait for you, and in fact you may not even have any cardinal traits at all. It's not a central trait, either, as being kind or unkind is not something that would really differentiate you from others.

But let's say there are very specific situations that bring out your kindness in ways that really do make you stand out. You have a soft spot for troubled teens, perhaps, maybe because you were once one yourself. You give big to causes that help these young men and women when the holidays roll around. Perhaps kindness, after all, is one of your traits, but it's a secondary one. It may not manifest when you are jostling to get a seat on the subway or when you are giving the finger to someone in traffic. But it is there in certain situations, and that makes it a trait, in some form.

The same could be true for any number of other traits, from being funny to being energetic, from being fearful to being orderly. Only a few of us are defined completely by one cardinal trait, one that can make us a caricature like Scrooge or Mother Teresa. But for most of us, different layers of traits add up and make us who we are.

Allport's categories of values also tell us something about how we compare to others. Our values not only reflect what we believe to be important in life but also might help explain why we are drawn to different professional fields or set particular goals to be achieved. People with *theoretical* values are on a search for truth and may become scientists or philosophers. They investigate and analyze, to try to better understand the foundations of what is real in this life. People who tend toward *economic* values emphasize practicality; they want to create things of use and are utilitarian. They may become concerned with the accumulation of wealth. The *aesthetic*-valuing person places importance on experiencing harmony and beauty and is clearly more likely to be engaged in the creative arts as a career or as a side job. He or she seeks symmetry and grace and may sometimes value stylistic expression more than truth. People oriented toward *social* values are most interested in other human beings and relationships. They are focused on connectedness among people and are likely to be found in altruistic types of jobs that emphasize community or emotional connection. Allport's definition of *political* values says, perhaps cynically, that they involve a desire for power. Maybe power comes through an actual career in politics, or maybe someone is in a different industry altogether. But even in the latter case, the person who values power will be found acting in a way that is concerned with becoming a leader. And those with *religious* values seek unity, trying to find the way they fit into the universe as a whole and to understand not only their part within it but also the ways in which everything in life, and perhaps the cosmos, fits together.

What have you chosen to devote your life to? Or, at least, what have you chosen to devote the next few years to? What values lead you to be motivated to achieve certain goals? Perhaps you see yourself in some of these constructs, or you see yourself as a blend of two or more. Maybe early in your life you were driven by one set of values—let's say economic values, because they had long been instilled in you, given the need to put food on the table above all else. You spent your first couple of adult decades in middle management, comforted by your steady paycheck and your predictable life. But in mid-adulthood, you discovered volunteer work or painting or spirituality, and you suddenly found yourself driven by a different set of values altogether. With respect to Allport's theory of functional autonomy, the beauty of this is that we have the freedom to change ourselves midstream.

Raymond Cattell

BORN 1905, Hilltop, England

DIED 1998, Honolulu, Hawaii

Educated at King's College, London

BIG IDEA

Raymond Cattell is not to be confused with James McKeen Cattell, born 45 years earlier, one of the first psychology professors in the United States and a researcher who developed some early measures of intelligence. Raymond Cattell also made great strides in intelligence research but is best known for his work on the psychology of personality. One of his biggest contributions is the **16PF**, a trait measure based on 16 personality factors that he saw as defining human beings. He used a lexical approach, starting with the language used to define traits, and built on Gordon Allport's work.

Cattell believed that there are three major sources of data for personality traits, and that in order for a trait to be substantiated, it must be corroborated by information from all three sources. Life data (**L data**) is the life record—information that can be gleaned from others and from one's interactions with society, such as court records and peer ratings. Questionnaire data (**Q data**) involves self-reports of individual traits. **T data** (experimental data) involves objective personality measures obtained in experimental settings where one might not even be aware that one's personality is what is being assessed.

This latter idea—that it should not necessarily be obvious what a measure is assessing—is important because personality measures can be plagued by the problem of **self-serving bias**. We want to view ourselves as good people and probably also get the person doing the personality assessment to believe that we are good. And this can make us less than accurate in our answers. This is a common flaw of the many nonempirical personality tests that circulate on social media: How honest are you? What is your biggest emotional strength? What *Big Bang Theory* character are you? It is very easy to answer questions in a way that makes us look good; after all, few of us want to describe ourselves as being dishonest or devoid of emotional strength. So we might be inclined to fake it a bit, on the test or perhaps also in terms of how we view ourselves.

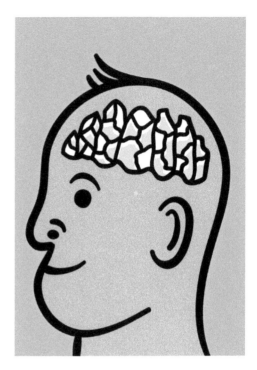

Tests that have a high degree of what is called **face validity** can be particularly susceptible to this kind of fakery. When a personality test is very clear about what it's looking for, the temptation to make yourself look good can be particularly strong and also easy to indulge. More sophisticated personality measures, however, are less obvious about what they are measuring and thus make it more difficult to game the system.

Cattell sampled children, adolescents, and adults, and he collected data across several different cultures, from the United States to Brazil, New Zealand, India, and Japan. He used **factor analysis** to identify **surface traits** and **source traits**. *Surface traits* is the term he used for specific, more superficial descriptors of a person—characteristics that might come and go in different situations— whereas the term *source traits* denotes more fundamental characteristics that represent a true factor of the personality. The 16 personality traits of the 16PF are all source traits, and Cattell identified them as warmth, reasoning, emotional stability, dominance, liveliness, rule-consciousness, social boldness, sensitivity, vigilance, abstractedness, privateness, apprehension, openness to change, self-reliance, perfectionism, and tension. Cattell was likely the first to use a computer to perform factor analysis on personality traits, which significantly increased the volume of data he could use in his calculations. The precision with which he conducted

Raymond Cattell's trait theories and factor analysis led to further attempts to explore psychological characteristics and break them down into groups of salient features. His work was a forerunner of the later Big Five theory, which reduces the traits to extraversion, agreeableness, neuroticism/emotional stability, openness to experience, and conscientiousness.

WHAT ABOUT ME?

Many online dating sites include built-in personality assessments. But, as Cattell's 16PF shows, personality factors, even when they can be clearly identified, are a matter of degree. Even if we admire one of a potential partner's traits, such as sensitivity or self-reliance, too much or too little of that trait might become a problem—someone who is sensitive might also be overemotional at times, and someone who is self-reliant might also sometimes have trouble being vulnerable enough to sustain an intimate relationship. And, of course, it's always important to remember that the human urge to embellish, especially on a dating site, together with our human inability to be completely objective in assessing ourselves, means that the personality description in someone's profile is not necessarily the whole story.

his calculations and derived his measures was well regarded, and it pushed forward the field of **psychometrics**—psychological measurement—quite significantly.

Cattell's theories also have something to say about intelligence. He differentiated between two different types of intelligence: crystallized and fluid. **Crystallized intelligence** includes information that you have accumulated over time—all the data and knowledge derived from your education that has solidified (perhaps not totally) within your brain. **Fluid intelligence** includes the ability to do something with that information; it is adaptive and involves the ability to find solutions to problems in the moment.

Abraham Maslow

BORN 1908, Brooklyn, New York

DIED 1970, Menlo Park, California

Educated at City College of New York and the University of Wisconsin

BIG IDEA

Abraham Maslow's humanistic theories have permeated our culture and provided much food for thought about how we strive to be the best people we can be and about what we are capable of. Though he started out as a behaviorist and studied attachment behavior under Harry Harlow, the theories that Maslow is most known for are not empirical in nature, which is the most frequent criticism leveled against them. Nonetheless, his ideas about human needs, values, and achievement, and his concept of **self-actualization**, have formed a foundation for further study of how we fulfill our potential as human beings.

Maslow is primarily known for what he called the **hierarchy of needs**, with the principle of self-actualization sitting atop the hierarchy. He was first inspired by his mentors, the anthropologist Ruth Benedict and the Gestalt psychologist Max Wertheimer, not because they studied self-actualization but because he felt that they were the very human representation of it. To Maslow, they were professionally and personally accomplished, kind, and caring people who seemed to have a purpose greater than themselves. Maslow's previous research under Harlow had shown him that needs can come in degrees, with various needs superseding each other (if you can't breathe, you're not worried about thirst; if you're dying of dehydration, you're not worried about lack of shelter). Maslow expanded the concept of needs to include not just biological needs but social, emotional, and psychological ones as well. The hierarchy can be represented as a ladder, with every need from the bottom rung up requiring satisfaction before progress up the ladder can be made.

The bottom level of the ladder, or hierarchy, represents physiological needs, everything from oxygen to sleep to vitamins, from getting rid of waste to avoiding pain and having sex. The next level up represents needs related to security and safety—things like protection, stability, and perhaps structure and order. Next up are needs related to love and belonging, which include affection and interpersonal relationships, a sense of community, and perhaps finding a partner or a meaningful career. The esteem-related needs are next: admiration, attention, recognition, and appreciation, and also self-respect, independence, freedom, confidence, and a sense of competence.

All the aforementioned needs are what Maslow called "deficiency" needs, or **D-needs**, because if they aren't met, you feel compelled to fill those gaps. But once you satisfy them, you don't feel any extra motivation to go further. For instance, when you quench your thirst with a nice tall glass of ice water, you don't want to keep on going with even more water once you are fully satisfied.

Maslow also said that we can regress down the hierarchy in times of crisis (if a crime wave breaks out in your neighborhood, you will quickly become more concerned with safety and security all over again, friendships be darned). If you have a particularly severe or prolonged case of a need's not being met—long periods of hunger as a child, or going through abuse, for example—you might develop a fixation on that need for the rest of your life (a rather Freudian concept).

The top level of the hierarchy represents not the D-needs but what Maslow called the "being" needs, or **B-needs**. Maslow said that these needs are for things like goodness, truth, beauty, playfulness, aliveness, and unity. This is also the place where the drive for self-actualization comes into being. Unlike the D-needs, the B-needs are never truly met, but for those who have risen to this level, the B-needs continue to be motivating. Maslow studied biographies of famous and obscure people, observing trends and characteristics, and concluded that only about 1 in 50 of us ever get to the point of self-actualization. He said that people who are self-actualizing are realistic problem solvers, able to be alone with themselves but also to have meaningful intimate relationships. They are autonomous and not easily swayed by peer pressure or by the need to conform. They accept themselves and others, and they have a sense of humor that is not used aggressively. They can be spontaneous and unconcerned with calculating an image or putting on a persona. People who are self-actualizing, according to Maslow, have a sense of humility and respect; Maslow referred to their values as *democratic values*. He saw compassion and interest in other people as factors in human kinship and in a strong sense of ethics. Maslow's self-actualizers are creative and look at life as something to be discovered and appreciated, and though they aren't perfect, they are fully themselves and are able to be at peace with that. They tend to care more about the challenges they are striving to overcome or the problems they are solving than about being overly self-involved.

THEN WHAT?

Maslow's theories, which helped usher in the humanistic movement in psychology, can very well be considered to have laid the foundation for later work in the field of positive psychology, and for the general shift away from focusing solely on disorders and illness and toward also studying growth, joy, and fulfillment. Martin Seligman, one of the humanistic movement's leading contemporary researchers, was directly influenced by Maslow's work, which can also be seen to align somewhat with Viktor Frankl's work, although there are some notable differences (for example, Frankl felt that meaning can be found even in the most desperate situations, whereas Maslow maintained that lower-order needs must be met before someone can reach the stage of striving for self-actualization).

WHAT ABOUT ME?

Have you ever had a moment in your life when you felt that everything had clicked into place, even if that moment was fleeting? Perhaps it was when you witnessed an extraordinarily beautiful sunset on the vacation of a lifetime, or when you crossed a hard-won graduation stage or saw your sister declared cancer-free. Maybe it was a moment when something more mundane occurred—you watched your father joke around with your son, you felt gratitude from someone you had helped out, or you were struck by the beauty of some wildflowers on a highway median. These *peak experiences*, in Maslow's terminology, can pack quite an emotional (some would even say spiritual) punch. They often stick out as the visuals that propel us forward in life, the things we remember that give us a reason to keep going. Maslow argued that if you are having more and more of these, you are on the right track, as you are on the road to self-actualization.

Some believe that peak experiences have something in common with the concept of *flow*, first proposed by Mihaly Csikszentmihalyi. Flow is what you feel when you get "in the zone": You're focused and feeling good, absorbed enough in a task that other things don't seem to matter. You are optimally both challenged and relaxed. You may be washing dishes, signing an executive order, or doing anything in between, but time just passes—it's the opposite of watching the clock—and you are fulfilled in the moment.

Naturally, these are among some of life's most positive experiences. When was the last time you had one? Or are you lucky enough that you have them quite regularly? Clearly, not just luck is involved. People striving to self-actualize, Maslow argued, are much more likely to make them happen. And who, exactly, is self-actualizing? Maslow's historical examples aside, is there someone in your life whom you've always admired? A loving aunt, a wise and giving mentor, a serene and supportive friend? Have you ever tried to put your finger on exactly what it is about this person that seems so inspiring? Maybe you've even tried to be like him or her and found it impossible. There's a quality there that defies easy description. Understanding what makes people like that who they are is more an art than a science.

It is these rare people whom we might see as self-actualizing, and they likely inspire awe in us. But what is ironic is that, by the very definition of self-actualization, they are just being themselves. Mimicking them or shape-shifting ourselves into some facsimile will get us nowhere, as Maslow maintained that they are acting from principles that truly come from within, without calculation or artifice. What does it mean to be true to yourself? What are the things you cherish most? The pursuit of beauty, harmony, and truth through art, music, or writing? The challenge of reaching new milestones of stamina and strength and getting the endorphin rush of exercise? Maslow might very well say that we have to look inside ourselves first, and that any of these things represents s valid step in the process of self-actualization if that step is really aligned with our values. There is no road map. There is no perfection. And, most inspiring of all, there is no finished product—that's why Maslow's term is *self-actualizing* rather than *self-actualized*.

Hans Eysenck

BORN 1916, Berlin, German Empire

DIED 1997, London, England

Educated at University College,
London

BIG IDEA

Hans Eysenck had myriad interests within psychology, and his prolific writings include treatises on intelligence testing, behavior therapy, physiology, and genetics. But his biggest legacy remains in the field of personality psychology, where he used empirical and statistical techniques like factor analysis to identify certain personality dimensions that help describe how we differ from each other.

Factor analysis involves taking large amounts of data and looking for cohesive categories—factors—that are found to be statistically salient. One does this by examining the correlation between every single pair of data points and seeing which ones tend to go together. Factor analysis became a popular source of study for personality psychologists and often started with the language that has been developed to refer to personality traits. You could take lists and lists of words that we use and start to assess which ones tend to overlap in terms of how they describe someone. *Well-mannered* and *polite* might correlate with each other rather closely, for example, whereas *affectionate* might overlap some but also speak to a different quality altogether, and *kind* might be in the middle of all of them.

Eysenck dared to narrow personality traits down to only two main factors, which he believed to encompass who

---

we are: *introversion/extraversion* and *neuroticism*. The former involves characteristics that he expanded upon after the work of Carl Jung, even though Eysenck was a very forceful opponent of psychoanalysis. The latter factor, neuroticism, involves one's level of emotional stability (or emotional instability). Eysenck saw these two dimensions as independent of each other, and they could be viewed as intersecting axes, offering the ability to plot personality into different quadrants. And he gave each of those quadrants a name corresponding to the temperaments that had been identified by Hippocrates more than 2,000 years before: *melancholic* (prone to the blues), *choleric* (hotheaded), *phlegmatic* (calm and reserved), and *sanguine* (cheerful). Of course, in Hippocrates's definition, these personality types were directly attributable to the individualized levels of bodily fluids that people supposedly carry around: black bile, yellow bile, phlegm, and blood, respectively. Eysenck did not subscribe to that particular theory, but he recognized that physiology plays a role in personality, and he believed that such personality types tend to be genetically ingrained.

Eysenck looked toward biology to explore this concept further and to help explain how what was happening in our particular bodies can turn us into the types of people we are. For example, he hypothesized that neuroticism has to do with how sensitive the sympathetic nervous system is: Highly neurotic (or anxious) people, he said, have an

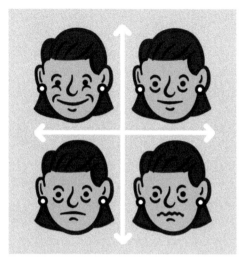

overactive sympathetic nervous system that goes into fight-or-flight mode at the slightest provocation. We've all felt the body preparing for action (or freezing in terror) in moments of fear—the heart rate increases, breathing gets faster, and the hair on the arms may stand on end.

Eysenck's theories of introversion and extraversion went beyond Jung's and into biology as well. According to Eysenck, this dimension involves **excitation** and **inhibition** and what we do to negotiate the balance between these two ends of the spectrum. To Eysenck, excitation meant increased alertness, with the brain at full attention. Inhibition was the opposite, with the brain trying to calm itself down by blocking out stimuli or even going to sleep. Eysenck said that the more extraverted someone is, the stronger his or her inhibition processes. That sounds counterintuitive, as we tend to think of inhibition in terms of being behaviorally inhibited—being too shy to talk to some-one, or being too anxious to express our true selves. But remember that Eysenck was talking about physiological inhi-bition, not behavioral inhibition—he was referring to how our bodies inhibit arousal—and so the higher the inhibi-tion, the greater the ability to keep from becoming overly anxious, and thus the greater the ability to attune to the outer world (like an extravert) without with-drawing into the self (like an introvert).

Eysenck's theory said that this is why the differences between extraverts and introverts are seen not just in how people react to other individuals but also in how they respond to their envi-ronment. Extraverts can often study in the presence of background noise without becoming overstimulated, per-haps even preferring some white noise. Extraverts, it has been suggested, also perform better with caffeine than intro-verts do and are happy to have a lot of information thrown at them when they're making decisions. This is all because it is harder to overtax their nervous sys-tems, and they have a higher threshold to reach before feeling overexcited.

Trait theories of personality are not without their detractors, and the ques-tion of how much personality trumps situational context is one that persists to this day (and underlies the differences between the psychology of personality and social psychology). Furthermore, the notion that genetic factors over-whelmingly cause these differences is

no longer as certain today. Eysencks's focus on genetics also led him down the controversial and disputed path of suggesting that racial differences in intelligence may be widespread and inherited. Nonetheless, Eysenck's use of statistical techniques and physiological findings to validate personality distinc-tions was a big step forward for the field.

After a period of focusing only on his main two personality factors, Eysenck realized that there might be samples of populations that he was not dipping into. So he collected data among those who were hospitalized in psychiatric institu-tions. Eventually this led to his adding the dimension of *psychoticism*, which to him meant aggressive, impulsive, and antisocial attributes. (This is not to be confused with the purer modern definition of psychosis, which refers more specifically to the experience of hallucination and delusions.)

THEN WHAT?

Eysenck's personality research paved the way for further exploration of physiology and behavior, and for further trait theories of personality. He was instrumental in arguing for the importance of genetic influ-ences on personality and for the impor-tance of measurement in psychological research. He also espoused some offensive and controversial views, such as the idea that the alignment of the planets at one's birth affects personality, and the notion that the development of cancer among smokers is less linked to cigarettes than to the interaction of smoking with personality and constitutional factors.

WHAT ABOUT ME?

When you think of your friends and loved ones, you may have a very good idea of how you would rate them in terms of introversion and extraversion, and emotional stability versus instability. As brief and simple as these two categories may seem, though, if you combined them to create the quadrants that Eysenck defined, you might be surprised by just how many characteristics they encompass.

The melancholic personality—high in instability and introversion—could be seen as quiet, pessimistic, rigid, and moody. Surely we know people like this. Some of them, though troubled, even seem to be particularly talented: brooding artists, tortured writers, singers who have been in a permanent dark phase. They are tuned in to their own thoughts, but living among those thoughts is not a particularly calm experience. Things are stormy. And yet they may retreat from the world, further into their own feelings, which might distress them enough to retreat even further and then, perhaps, find ways of expressing themselves to help with some of the distress.

Now let's visualize the choleric personality: high in both extraversion and instability. Here, the distress seen in the melancholic personality is turned outward. Maybe you know someone, a fully grown adult, who is prone to tantrums,

quick to anger, and chronically tense: one little slip-up from someone else, and such people blow their stacks. Perhaps they have chronic road rage or are prone to getting into online fights with people who disagree with them politically. Like melancholic personalities, such people are unstable—the storm inside them is brewing—but they are more externally oriented. They are extraverts, not in the sense of being charming and popular, but in the sense of always being focused outside themselves.

The phlegmatic personalities—high in introversion and low in instability—are not often raising people's hackles as the choleric type does, but they're also probably not often on people's radar. Attuned inward, and not particularly driven by bouts of emotion, they are likely rather quiet and unassuming. Eysenck was not particularly complimentary of this type (the sanguine type alone got a thumbs-up from him) in that he described phlegmatic personalities as also tending toward laziness and passivity. We all may know plenty of perfectly pleasant people in this category, but they tend not to be particularly noticeable. They might move slowly through life because they lack the jolt of varying emotions.

Finally, the sanguine personalities—high in extraversion and low in instability—are comfortable with themselves and not prone to outbursts. They are often optimistic and even bubbly, maintaining an even keel but being interested in the world around them. If you know any people like this, you've probably noticed that their social calendars are fairly full, in part because other people want to be around them.

Although we all know people who fit these types, it's important to remember that Eysenck recognized the dimensional nature of the traits represented by his quadrants; he delineated these four personality types along an x-y axis, so they touch each other, and it's possible for someone to be anywhere within a particular quadrant. In recent years, we have seen more of a focus on the undeserved bad rap that introverts get. It is true that in these groupings, Eysenck seems to have associated introversion a bit more with unhealthy qualities, perhaps because of its association with the physiological aspects of needing to tune out the world. Though we might tend to think of introversion more favorably today, Eysenck's types and their physiological underpinnings are a great starting point for thinking about what makes us tick.

Social Psychology

While personality psychology is concerned with individual differences in behavior that endure across situations (Jake is rigid and prone to anger, whether ordering in a restaurant or dealing with his children; Kaylee is conflict-avoidant, no matter the situation), social psychology focuses on the commonalities in behavior among all of us in specific situations. Why do people behave very differently in riots from how they act on their own? What is it about being in a group that makes us want to conform? How can people rise to power who are cruel and act against the interests of the people supporting them? Why is the hidden-camera genre, from *Candid Camera* to *Punk'd*, so extremely fascinating, and what does it say about the science of human behavior?

Social psychologists look not only at our interactions with each other but also at the ways in which the circumstances of our environments shape our behavior. Their experiments are often fascinating microcosms of human behavior, employing secret actors to behave as if they are part of an experiment, when in reality they are moving the action along. Social psychologists often focus on observable behaviors and draw conclusions about what the motivations for those behaviors might be. Some psychologists, including a few we'll discuss here, combine other fields of psychology—cognition, emotion, and personality—to more fully expand their theories.

Kurt Lewin

●—●

BORN 1890, Mogilno, Prussia,
German Empire

DIED 1947, Newtonville,
Massachusetts

Educated at the University of Berlin

BIG IDEA

Kurt Lewin is often credited with being
the original social psychologist. A keen
observer of people and culture, he suggested that it is neither nature nor nurture
alone, but instead the interaction between
the two, that accounts for who we are.
Some people have a vested interest in
believing that our genes are our destiny, or
that early life experiences all but cement
exactly who we will become. But think
about it—nature cannot exist without

nurture. Genetic destiny cannot become
manifest without the environment to
support it. If you have the genes for brown
eyes, but your biological mother developed an infection while she was pregnant
with you and that infection kept your eyes
from developing at all, then your eye-color
genes turned out not to matter after all.

The gap between genetic and environmental factors is not the only one
that Lewin helped bridge. He also wanted
to bring scientific scrutiny to everyday
behavior. The seeming trivialities of
day-to-day life had been ignored by many
theorists of his time, but in daily reality
Lewin saw profound clues to the essence
of what it means to be human, and he
deemed those clues worthy of research.
Naturally, it is this idea—that everyday
behavior can be assessed, studied, and
eventually understood—that forms the

crux of social psychology. The notion that science can explore everyday behavior was a breath of fresh air in a field that had often sought to devote itself only to more sophisticated questions.

According to Lewin's **field theory**, people are constantly reacting within the framework of themselves and their environment. Lewin explained it this way: Every psychological event depends both on the state of the individual involved and on the environment, although the relative importance of each factor is different in different cases. Though that can seem inexact, this philosophy lays out a beautiful conceptualization of how the principles of personality psychology and social psychology work in tandem. Certain social forces and situations are so strong as to overrule personality factors (a win for the social psychologists), whereas others do not exert enough influence to overcome the individual differences among us (a triumph for personality psychologists).

Lewin's equation is a more specific statement that behavior is a function of the characteristics a person carries around and of how those characteristics react to the environment. Lewin also used the term **life space** to describe the sum of the influences that act on a person at any given point in time. Individual influences themselves—memories, desires, sensations, and the like—are called *psychological facts*. Lewin posited that the older we get, the bigger our life space gets as we add not just new experiences but also our memories of those experiences. These

experiences can come back to influence us in quite meaningful ways later on.

Lewin also developed a theory of conflict that involves three specific subtypes:

» In an **approach-approach conflict**, we are trying to decide between two desirable goals.
» An **approach-avoidance conflict** involves only one goal, but it is one that simultaneously attracts and repels us.
» In an **avoidance-avoidance conflict**, we must choose between two options that are both repellent.

What Lewin theorized is that the closer we get to an individual choice or goal, the more extremely we feel its positive or negative qualities, and the more we are attracted or repelled. The approach-approach conflict is inherently unstable, making us act more quickly, as the closer we move to one of the goals, the more attracted we become, and since it is desirable, we go with it. The other two conflicts are inherently more stable, allowing us to be indecisive for longer as we move back and forth between being repelled and being attracted (approach-avoidance) or between two different ways of being repelled (avoidance-avoidance.)

Lewin looked beyond conflict within the individual to study conflict and cohesion within groups. The term *organizational development* sounds like a buzzword of the late 20th century—it practically reeks of whiteboards, memos, and squeaky chairs in conference rooms—but in the early decades of the 20th century Lewin was already developing theories within this field. He identified three different styles of workplace environment, or **leadership culture**:

» In a *democratic* leadership culture, all members of the organization feel like active participants, and there are no significant differences in status between leaders and nonleaders; this culture is associated with greater creativity and functionality than are found in the other two leadership cultures.

» An *autocratic* leadership culture has rigid leaders; followers feel less involved in organizational processes and are more likely to revolt than in the other two leadership cultures.

» In a *laissez-faire* leadership culture, the boundaries of leadership are less clear than in the other two leadership cultures; workers are less unified, and their work is less coherent.

Interestingly enough, Lewin originally derived these three leadership cultures from research conducted on 10-year-old boys—*Lord of the Flies*, anyone?

THEN WHAT?

By establishing a framework for how social forces affect behavior, Lewin set the stage for a new field entirely. His work in social psychology directly influenced other early pioneers, including Leon Festinger, whom Lewin mentored, and who went on to develop **social comparison theory** and the concept of **cognitive dissonance**.

And it was one of Lewin's supervisees, Bluma Zeigarnik, who first discovered that we tend to remember our unfinished tasks more clearly and for longer than we remember our finished tasks (this phenomenon is known as the *Zeigarnik effect*).

WHAT ABOUT ME?

As you get older, you may have the rather unsettling feeling that your birthday comes around more quickly with each passing year. Lewin's concept of the life space provides a framework for understanding this feeling. As you age, your life space grows; you continue to add experiences, memories, and still more experiences and more memories, expanding your emotional and mental reality. All the while, however, a year remains constant—it still has 365 days (366 in a leap year)—and so the percentage of your life that is accounted for by the year that has passed since your last birthday becomes smaller and smaller as time goes on. When you're 5 years old, the year that just passed accounts for 20 percent of your lifetime. By the time you're 25, the year that just passed accounts for only 4 percent of your lifetime, and by the time you're 90, the year that just passed accounts for only a little more than 1 percent of your lifetime. That's why time seems to move faster and faster from one birthday to the next.

Lewin's ideas around internal conflict, originally formulated in the early decades of the 20th century, still resonate decades later. Which Caribbean resort will you choose—the one with a swim-up bar, fine dining, hammocks galore, and fancy skewers of tropical fruit in each drink, or the other one that has all the same amenities? (That's an approach-approach conflict.) Should you leave an emotionally abusive relationship and opt for freedom and psychological health, or should you stay so you won't have to deal with your partner's reaction, sort out the logistics of a move, disentangle your finances from your partner's, and suffer an almost certain period of loneliness? (This is an approach-avoidance conflict.) When your boss gives you the choice between taking a pay cut or putting in 10 more hours per week, which option will you choose? (This is an avoidance-avoidance conflict.)

Leon Festinger

—●——●—

BORN 1919, New York City, New York

DIED 1989, New York City, New York

Educated at City College of New York and the University of Iowa

BIG IDEA

Leon Festinger was one of the most eminent psychologists of modern times, contributing theories to social psychology that have become pillars of the field. He was also a person of varied interests, eventually studying visual perception, history, and even archaeology, which, he argued, are as much about psychology as anything else.

Festinger's greatest theory, that of cognitive dissonance, says that when we have two simultaneous and seemingly incompatible thoughts, we will do what we can to minimize the discrepancy by adjusting our thoughts accordingly. We don't like the discomfort that the incompatibility creates, and so we are motivated to get rid of it, even if we have to change what we believe. These thoughts can involve our attitudes, our observations, or even our acknowledgment that we are engaging in certain behaviors. When the brain catches the discrepancy, we become uncomfortable. And so we search for a way to make the discrepancy go away.

Experiments that Festinger conducted showed that such an attitude change is even more likely when we feel that we have a choice about our actions, and when we are able to foresee the consequences. We are also more likely to accept responsibility for our behavior when we don't think that someone else is coercing us; and, having accepted responsibility for our behavior, we can feel the discomfort of cognitive dissonance when it turns out that our behavior isn't making a lot of sense, and so we force it to make sense.

The concept of cognitive dissonance also applies to situations in which we have to choose between two options. We want to convince ourselves that the choice we've made was correct, and so we increasingly view the option we chose as attractive, and we increasingly downgrade the choice we rejected, to bat away the dissonance of seeing it, too, as an attractive option. In fact, research shows this pattern in voting behavior—we hold our chosen candidates in higher esteem right after we vote for them than we did right before. We want to justify our decisions, to know that our attitudes and our behavior are aligned, and to avoid the discomfort of thinking that we should have chosen something or someone else.

Another area of Festinger's work that made great waves is social comparison theory. This theory says that we constantly try to assess our own characteristics as they compare to those of others, sizing ourselves up to see where we stand in terms of our values and abilities. And the more we identify with certain people, the more we care about how we measure up to them. This tendency can sometimes serve to bolster our opinions: "She believes that, and she's pretty much like me, so I should believe it too." Or it can make us choose the opposite opinion: "I can't stand her. If she supports that candidate, I probably

shouldn't." Sometimes it serves to help us define our abilities: "Everyone else seems to be out of breath walking up these stairs, so I must not be in such bad shape after all." We may feel unsure or downright confused when we're alone with our own thoughts or actions, but when we can justify or validate them by comparing ourselves to others, we feel much better, and we convince ourselves that we have a more accurate evaluation of ourselves.

Festinger was also the first to conclusively establish how much proximity matters in the development of friendships, and how the everyday familiarity and random interactions that come from simply being near someone may matter more than many other factors in terms of how likely we are to develop a friendship.

Sometimes we get lucky. Perhaps the colleagues and roommates we fell in with are good people. But if proximity draws us into a friendship that turns out not to have been the best choice, then the power of proximity looks less benign.

THEN WHAT?

The concept of cognitive dissonance led to all kinds of new research on interactions between attitudes and behavior. Festinger's work directly influenced later psychologists who studied decision making. Among his students were the notable social psychologists Elliot Aronson and Stanley Schachter (the latter studied how physiological arousal can send us searching for an explanation that determines how we label our emotions).

WHAT ABOUT ME?

Let's say you've spent all night waiting in line to get tickets to the premiere of a long-awaited movie. Once inside the theater, you settle in with your popcorn. But as you watch the movie, you start to notice that the special effects, the dialogue, and the acting are all underwhelming. You are beginning to understand that you chose, of your own free will, to put yourself through considerable sacrifice in exchange for getting to see this terrible film. Cognitive dissonance has struck. What will you do now? Leon Festinger would say that you'll try to relieve the dissonance in any way you can. You can't change the fact that you spent all night waiting in line, but you can change what you think of the movie. "I was up all night," you'll tell yourself, "so I'm probably just tired. The movie's not so bad. Actually, it's pretty good."

More fascinating is a cultural phenomenon that Festinger studied methodologically—the doomsday cult. For his 1956 book *When Prophecy Fails*, coauthored with Henry W. Riecken, Festinger infiltrated the Seekers, a group headed by a Chicago-area housewife whom Festinger called Marian Keech. She foretold a great flood that would end the world on December 21, 1954, but not before a flying saucer swept her and her followers off to the planet Clarion. Festinger waited and watched with the Seekers as the hour of the Earth's demise came and went. Finally Keech announced that the Earth was to be spared after all. Most of her followers, instead of cutting their losses, reaffirmed their faith and doubled down on proselytizing—a clear example of cognitive dissonance in action.

Stanley Milgram

—•—•—

BORN 1933, New York City, New York

DIED 1984, New York City, New York

Educated at Queens College and Harvard University

BIG IDEA

Stanley Milgram's work in social psychology spanned several areas. The first, though not nearly as infamous as his later research on obedience to authority, involved connectedness among people. In a noteworthy study, he randomly sent packages to 160 people in Nebraska and asked each of them to send the package on to a stranger in Boston who had an unlisted address. To complete the task, the package recipients were allowed to use only intermediaries whom they did know, but who they thought would take them one step closer to getting the packages to their intended recipients in Boston. Remarkably, many of the packages did reach their targets in Boston, with the help of only a few intermediaries. The average number of intermediaries was 5.5, and thus was born the notion of six degrees of separation.

But by far Milgram's best-known work involved obedience to authority. His interest in this topic came from the horrified "whys" and "hows" following the Nazis' extermination of 11 million people in the Holocaust, including 6 million Jews. What happens to make a seemingly healthy, moral, "normal" individual go along with the planned annihilation of his or her fellow human beings? What does "just following orders" really mean, and how far can it go as an explanation of sickening, violent behavior? The trial

of Adolf Eichmann, who oversaw the murder of millions of Jews in the Nazi gas chambers, was well publicized across the world in 1961. And that was likely a direct catalyst for Milgram's most famous series of experiments, conducted a few months later and showing that even ordinary people can be induced to harm other people whom they don't even know, especially when an apparently legitimate authority figure tells them to do so.

Milgram believed that cultures all around the world stress obedience to authority, to the point where people can come to feel like agents acting on behalf of other people's desires, and that the sense

of personal responsibility for actions can begin to disappear. He also illuminated the role of psychological distance between actions and their consequences. The more emotionally removed people feel from the consequences of their behavior, the more they feel that they are just cogs in a machine, carrying out actions that they may or may not even agree with.

But why would any of us do things that we don't agree with, especially when they involve hurting others? Milgram posited that it becomes easier when we stick our heads in the proverbial sand. We do our best to blind ourselves to the reality of the emotional and physical

KEY EXPERIMENT In 1961, Stanley Milgram was a professor at Yale University. He placed a newspaper ad that offered Connecticut residents $4.50 per hour for their participation in an experiment. Respondents were told that they would be involved in a study exploring the relationship between punishment and learning.

In this series of experiments, the participants (formerly called subjects, a term now considered problematic for its connotations of powerlessness) were all men, and they went through the experiment in pairs, though one of the two men was always a confederate (that is, an actor who appeared to be just like his counterpart but was actually in on the experiment). The participant and the confederate appeared to have been assigned their roles of teacher and learner randomly, but in truth the distribution of roles was always rigged so that the real participant was always the teacher. The learner (the confederate) was a mild-mannered middle-aged man in professional dress. With the teacher looking on, an experimenter strapped the learner to a chair and attached electrodes to his wrists.

In one version of the experiment, the experimenter then led the teacher into a different room, where the teacher was unable to see the learner and could communicate with him only by way of a loudspeaker. The experimenter then showed the teacher a shock generator. It had 30 switches, each one corresponding to a point along a spectrum of severity (15 to 450 volts), and each one labeled: (1) slight shock near the beginning, (2) very strong shock at 135 volts, (3) intense shock, (4) extreme-intensity shock, (5) danger—severe shock, and, finally and ominously, (6) just XXX at the two highest levels. Of course, the shock generator was fake, and it produced no shocks, but the teacher did not know this. The experimenter gave the teacher a 45-volt shock as a demonstration of how being shocked would feel. That was only three levels up from the beginning of the spectrum (slight shock), but it was clearly uncomfortable.

The experimenter instructed the teacher to present a list of word pairs to the learner, who in turn was supposed to remember the correct associations.

»

Then the teacher was to test the learner, and when the learner gave an incorrect response, the teacher was instructed to shock him by flipping one of the labeled switches. The teacher was also instructed to increase the level of shock by 15 volts with each new error on the part of the learner.

Prerecorded audio masqueraded as the learner's real-time responses, and so the learner's responses were the same for every teacher-learner pair. When the level of the shocks administered by the teacher reached about 120 volts, the prerecorded voice shouted that the shocks were too painful. At 150 volts, the voice demanded release from the experiment. At 300 volts, the voice screamed that no further answers would be given, and succeeding shocks were met with complete silence. If the teacher balked at proceeding, the experimenter prompted him to go on, using a series of increasingly imperative statements that began with "Please continue" and ended with "You have no other choice; you must go on." If the teacher balked four times, the experiment was ended.

About 65 percent of the teachers obeyed the experimenter all the way to the end, even when the learner had mentioned at the beginning of the experiment that he had a heart condition. Results varied with different conditions. For example, when the experimenter was not a white-coated investigator but a younger person, fewer people obeyed. There was also much less obedience when the learner remained in view of the teacher.

It is worth noting that the infliction of psychological harm on the participants—many of whom expressed distress both during and after the experiment, believing that they had hurt someone—has raised ethical concerns about the experiment itself. It is quite safe to say that such an experiment would no longer be allowed to take place at a major academic institution. And not just ethical criticisms have been leveled at Milgram's research in the decades since these experiments. Methodological concerns have also been expressed, including certain researchers' criticism that some of the participants appear to have figured out that the scenario was not real.

experience of the person we are hurting. In fact, in our minds, the victim of our mistreatment may become less a person than an object—and we, too, cease to be thinking, feeling persons and instead become agents carrying out a task. This is dehumanization, and Milgram showed just how far it can go in making us willing to hurt people. And if someone who wants us to harm others can come up with a lofty rationalization for that behavior, we find ourselves all the more able to justify our actions. Milgram revealed a slippery slope—if gradations are offered along the path of doing harm, then hurting another person a little bit appears to pave the way to hurting the person a lot.

Milgram's theories exemplify the central tenet of social psychology—that the situations we find ourselves in can very much determine how we behave and even get us to behave in ways that are out of line with what we normally would do (or think we would do). Needless to say, Milgram's findings are extremely unsettling. Nevertheless, by provocatively asking just how far human beings can be induced to go, he began our exploration of the forces of authority and the urge to obey, and of how to help people stand up to those forces.

THEN WHAT?

Stanley Milgram's findings spurred decades of study about the strength of social and situational factors in inducing people to do startling things. His findings particularly inspired Philip Zimbardo,

who later conducted the Stanford Prison Experiment. Ethical concerns raised by Milgram's experimental research led to stricter regulation of psychological research and to a greater focus on protecting human participants.

WHAT ABOUT ME?

A particularly eerie *Twilight Zone* episode from 1986 illustrates the relative ease of inflicting damage on people we don't know and can't see. The episode, titled "Button, Button" and based on a short story by Richard Matheson, involves a couple in desperate financial circumstances. They are visited by a mysterious stranger, Mr. Steward, who is carrying a box. He tells them that if they press a button inside the box, they will receive $200,000, but they will also become responsible for the death of someone whom they don't know. The husband rejects the idea, but the wife eventually succumbs to the urge, rationalizing that the person about to die may be someone old and near death anyway. She presses the button. The next day, Mr. Steward returns and gives them the money. When the woman asks what will happen to the box, he tells her it will be reprogrammed, and that it will be offered to someone whom they don't know. And he looks her in the eye to make sure she understands exactly what she's done.

Or consider the TV series *Breaking Bad*. One of its most riveting and disturbing aspects is how an apparently ordinary high school science teacher, Walter White, eventually morphs into a heartless, murderous drug kingpin. He begins by selling crystal meth to ensure his family's financial stability after what he assumes will be his certain death from lung cancer. But as he progressively gains power and solidifies his earnings, he becomes farther and farther removed from the moral person we originally took him to be. He doesn't go from 0 to 60 in a week; it takes him years. But with each step he takes, the next becomes easier and less shocking.

None of us wants to think that we would push through someone's desperate screams and inflict unbearable pain on him simply because he didn't complete a task correctly. Just as the majority of American adults consider themselves better-than-average drivers—when, mathematically speaking, that can't possibly be the case—most of us are willing to give ourselves the benefit of the doubt when it comes to the strength of our moral values and our ability to resist an order to harm another human being. Our **illusory superiority** prompts us to judge ourselves more leniently than we judge others and to see ourselves as better than they are.

And yet Milgram's series of experiments revealed that most people, in certain conditions, will act in ways they probably don't personally believe are right. This is the norm, not the exception. But even though this reality could keep us awake at night, it is more reassuring, and insightful, to delve more deeply into how and why this is the case. As Milgram showed, the more we can distance ourselves from the reality of the suffering that our actions cause (or at least don't prevent), the less bothered by the suffering we will be. Even if you are a dog lover, if someone approached you on the street and told you that there are thousands of dogs in shelters and asked if you wanted to adopt one, you'd probably say, "Not today" and keep on walking, but it's much harder to say no to a shelter dog who is looking you right in the eye. Savvy nonprofits know that if they can show you the real-life human effects of your donation in a meaningful, personal way, they have a better shot at getting your compassion and empathy to kick in, and that your motivation to do the right thing is more likely to follow.

David Rosenhan

BORN 1929, Jersey City, New Jersey

DIED 2012, Palo Alto, California

Educated at Yeshiva College and
Columbia University

BIG IDEA

David Rosenhan, with one provocative,
controversial experiment—its results
were published in the journal *Science* in
1973, under the title "On Being Sane in
Insane Places"—pierced the bubble of
prestige that had come to envelop the
field of psychiatric care. He sent mentally healthy participants to 12 psychiatric institutions, where the participants
reported to admitting staff that they had
been hearing voices. The hospitals then
diagnosed the participants—mostly with
schizophrenia, one of the most serious
psychiatric conditions—and admitted
them for treatment. A striking aspect of
Rosenhan's experiment was its demonstration that when someone is given a psychiatric diagnosis—even, as in the case of the
participants, when the diagnosis is false—
it becomes a lens through which others
see every facet of the person's behavior,
even behavior that is completely normal.
Rosenhan challenged, in a major way, the
validity and reliability of how psychiatric
hospitals arrive at diagnoses, and he asked
what hospital staff is really willing to see
when looking at patients. He argued that
the psychiatric setting itself can become
an environment that promotes insanity
rather than sanity. He showed that those
who work in psychiatric institutions, from
orderlies to head psychiatrists, are prone
not only to label healthy people as sick but

also to label sick people as healthy. Perhaps most important of all, he showed that once someone is labeled with a diagnosis, it tends to become what he called "sticky," a defining declaration of insanity, even when the person shows no behavior that fits the diagnosis.

How, then, should we define abnormal behavior? If the difference between sanity and insanity can be so hard to quantify, what are the true markers of abnormality? In 1988, Rosenhan and Martin Seligman proposed seven parameters of abnormality; none, by itself, automatically means that a person's behavior should or will be deemed abnormal, but the more the behavior conforms to these parameters, the more likely it is that the behavior is or will become abnormal:

» *Suffering*, of course, is clear—the person is in distress.
» *Maladaptiveness* means that something about the person's behavior is getting in the way of his or her ability to meet goals or go through daily life.
» *Vivid/unconventional behavior* emphasizes how much the person's behavior differs from that of others.
» *Unpredictability/loss of control* may include inappropriate or erratic behavior.
» *Irrationality/incomprehensibility* involves an element of behavior whose motivation defies clear explanation.
» *Observer discomfort* refers to the unease that those watching this behavior will feel.

» *Violation of moral/ideal standards* occurs when the behavior does not fall within the established values of society.

Of course, some of these seven parameters may be matters for subjective judgment, but they paint a picture of the axes that we should, and tend to, think along when we discuss abnormality. They also offer more nuanced explanations of abnormality than can be found in the *DSM-5*.

THEN WHAT?

The publication of David Rosenhan's article "On Being Sane in Insane Places" shook up the field of psychiatry. It opened a discussion about the weaknesses of the medical model of treatment and about the potential biases of mental health care providers. It highlighted the dangers of overpathologizing and directly influenced various attempts at reform. Though Rosenhan's marquee experiment is no doubt what made his name in the field, he also did groundbreaking work at the intersection of psychological practice and the law. For example, he used techniques from the field of experimental psychology to look at how well jurors followed court-ordered instructions to ignore inadmissible evidence.

WHAT ABOUT ME?

What comes to mind when you read the following words?

» Schizophrenic
» Bulimic

» Manic-depressive
» Alcoholic

Do you read them as adjectives? If so, to whom are they attached? Imagine the people who are described by these adjectives. Imagine them all sitting together at a table. Is there yelling? Agitation? Are they in group therapy together? Are they locked up in a hospital? Or—imagine this—could they be family members sitting together and laughing warmly as they enjoy Thanksgiving dinner?

Now imagine a professor who has overcome schizophrenia. Imagine an artist who has had bouts of bulimia. Imagine a scientist with a history of bipolar disorder. Imagine a retired banker who has triumphed over alcoholism. Now we get a little more nuance, don't we? Maybe you see a man lecturing to an auditorium of rapt students, or a woman greeting guests at the opening of her sculpture exhibit, or a man doing card tricks for his grandchildren and saying, "No, thank you" when someone offers him a beer. Now these people are starting to look a little more human. But they've never *not* been human! Every single person in a therapy group or a psych ward or an AA meeting or at that Thanksgiving table has the same amount of humanity. Every person we meet and see is, by definition, a human being, but their humanity seems to wax and wane according to the labels we initially apply to them—and when we slap on the label of a mental health disorder, their humanity seems drastically diminished. We even turn adjectives— *schizophrenic*, *bulimic*, *manic-depressive*, *alcoholic*—into nouns, as if these nouns could actually encompass individual people themselves. Our language shows us that we're often more interested in a disorder than in the person who suffers from it. But this is a flawed way of thinking. That's why I teach my students, on the first day of class, that someone is a *person with schizophrenia* rather than *a schizophrenic*, and so on. When we put the person before the label, we can more easily remember his or her humanity, which hasn't disappeared just because he or she is suffering from a psychiatric illness.

Elliot Aronson

—•——•—

BORN 1932, Chelsea, Massachusetts

Educated at Brandeis University,
Wesleyan University, and Stanford
University

BIG IDEA

Elliot Aronson is a beloved name in psychology, and his vast career—stretching to our own time—has helped shape the direction of psychology, especially social psychology, in myriad ways. There is only one person in the history of the American Psychological Association who has won all its top awards—for research, for writing, and for teaching. That person is Elliot Aronson.

The development of the **jigsaw classroom** is perhaps his greatest accomplishment. For more than four decades, it has proved able to reduce student conflict and increase cooperation, learning, and motivation. It was first used in 1971, when one of Aronson's former students, then superintendent of public schools in Austin, Texas, was brainstorming ways to help lessen racial strife after desegregation. Aronson came up with the idea of dividing children in grades four through six into small groups, each one with a mix of kids from diverse backgrounds, and creating the objective for them to work together as a whole, with each individual serving the specific role of researching a certain concept and teaching it to the others. In order for everyone to be able to do well on later tests, it was clearly necessary for all of them to work together as a group. This arrangement brought resentment at first, but acceptance eventually followed. And then the groups really started paying off—signs of prejudice declined. And, compared to children in traditional learning situations, students in the jigsaw classrooms learned more effectively and showed more liking for each other, more liking for school, and greater self-esteem.

Over the ensuing decades, the implantation of jigsaw classrooms grew significantly. Additional benefits were found, such as reduced absenteeism, increased enjoyment of learning, and even better test scores. What sets the jigsaw classroom apart from traditional classroom setups is just how active each student must be within the group, as opposed to how passive learning can be in typical classrooms. It's also different in terms of how interconnected each student's role is with that of every other individual. There is less attention wasted on competition because all the students, in order to do well themselves, need the others to do well, too.

In a simple but effective way, the jigsaw classroom also safeguards against underperformers bringing down the group. For example, if a class is learning about the instruments in a symphony orchestra, then within every jigsaw group is a person assigned to strings, a different person assigned to woodwinds, a different one to percussion, and so on. During the initial research process, before the individual students present their assigned topics to their jigsaw groups, individual members across all the jigsaw groups who have matching roles get together in "expert" groups. All the students assigned to percussion, for example, will meet, rehearse, and compare notes.

By the time those students go back to their jigsaw groups to teach, their work has been strengthened and has had some oversight, and underperforming students have had the benefit of specific collaboration and support to improve what they will present to their groups. The teacher gets to play a facilitative role through all of it. The cooperative nature of the jigsaw classroom decreases the competition that sometimes exists between high achievers and also reduces resentment on the part of those who tend to feel left behind by the highest-achieving students. All the while, interpersonal skills and relationships are building.

Another of Aronson's big ideas was the **pratfall effect**. He showed that committing a blunder can influence someone's likability in very interesting ways, depending on whether the person who commits the blunder is or is not generally perceived as competent. People who are generally perceived as competent become more likable and attractive after a minor goof-up (such as spilling coffee); the blunder can be seen as endearing. Aronson has posited that this is probably because perfection can be intimidating and can make someone less relatable. Someone already perceived to be incompetent, however, is hurt by making an additional mistake—we likely just use it as further evidence for the negative opinion we already hold of him or her.

Aronson conducted several other classic studies that looked at how and why we like each other. One showed that we are bound to like someone more if that person starts off disliking us, and then

The jigsaw classroom continues to be implemented in many educational settings. Elliot Aronson further explored and expanded cognitive dissonance theory, including research that looked at how we resolve feelings of hypocrisy—and at how doing so can make people more likely to act in healthier ways, as in using condoms to reduce the risk of sexually transmitted illnesses after having had the role of teaching others about safe sex. His work has inspired further applications of social psychology to societal challenges, such as the use of peer pressure in energy conservation.

WHAT ABOUT ME?

Aronson's jigsaw classroom has been shown to have benefits in a wide range of school settings, even those with no overt racial conflict. Think about your school experience as an adolescent. Bullying, cliques, social anxiety, tension between teachers and students—these seem to be fundamental to the teen and even preteen experience, even for students who generally do well. But collaboration toward a shared goal appears to be helpful in all these situations. The evidence says that when diverse children come together for a common goal—rich kids and poor kids, athletes and artists, computer whizzes and class clowns—they like each other more, and they also do better at meeting educational goals.

grows to like us, than if the person has liked us from the beginning. This effect has to do with what has become known as the **gain-loss theory of attraction**, and it probably occurs because when we feel that we have won people over, it increases our good feelings about them. Aronson has also demonstrated that people are more committed to a group if they have to suffer significantly in order to be admitted, an effect that further illustrates the cognitive dissonance theory originated by Aronson's mentor, Leon Festinger.

Many consider Aronson's textbook *The Social Animal* the best social psychology text of all time. First published in 1972, it is currently in its 11th edition.

Aronson has argued that the jigsaw classroom can even play a significant role in preventing school violence. Those who commit violent acts at school are often socially isolated and consider themselves persecuted by bullies and cliques. Rejection, shame, and humiliation are frequent themes among those who act out. The types of gains shown in the jigsaw classroom, in terms of improving relationships between students of different backgrounds, can probably go a long way toward reducing isolation, rejection, and the sense of being an outsider.

As for the pratfall effect, we often see this play out in our attitudes toward celebrities. Those who are thought of as maintaining an impenetrable field of perfection often develop a reputation for being somewhat annoying. But if a celebrity is generally deemed good at what she does but is prone to the occasional goof-up, we tend to like her even more. We can see this effect with the literal pratfalls of Jennifer Lawrence.

And what about the gain-loss theory of attraction? Let's say that one of your bosses is particularly gruff and hard to please. He doesn't give you great feedback, and you feel that he may even have an unfairly negative opinion of you. At some point, you do a particularly great presentation, or just make a great joke that he loves, and now he seems to really like you. The good feedback starts coming, and he is warmer and much more interested in you than he was before. You've triumphed! Meanwhile, the boss who has always been complimentary of you starts to fade from your interest. You want to please this other boss instead, more than anything. You know that the boss who has always liked you is a sure bet to keep liking of you, but now the apple of your eye during your PowerPoint presentations is the boss who was formerly gruff toward you. This dynamic often seems to play out with teenagers as well. Let's say Colin has generally been ignored by the most popular set. But now, for whatever reason, the reigning king of his high school takes a liking to Colin, buddying around with him. Colin used to scoff at the popular kids, but now he thinks King Popular walks on water. Meanwhile, the friend who was always there for Colin from the beginning looks downright bland and lackluster by comparison.

Philip Zimbardo

—•——•—

BORN 1933, New York City, New York

Educated at Brooklyn College and Yale University

BIG IDEA

For several decades, Philip Zimbardo has been a colorful presence in social psychology. He is best known as the principal investigator in the Stanford Prison Experiment, a 1971 study whose extreme results are still breathlessly discussed some 45 years later.

The experiment and Zimbardo's analysis of the results are stark examples, like Stanley Milgram's experiments, of just how far environmental conditions can go in shaping our behavior. While Milgram's work highlighted obedience to authority, Zimbardo showed the importance of social roles—how taking on the persona of someone in power, or someone without any power at all, seems to drastically affect behavior. Like Milgram, Zimbardo showed that even the most seemingly psychologically healthy people can act with extreme cruelty, and that people with a wide range of personality traits are prone to such behavior. Zimbardo found that participants who were given the role of prison guard began to act inhumanely and, as some would argue, even sadistically. Those in the role of prisoner grew distressed, disconnected, and angry. Conflict between the two groups grew so severe that Zimbardo had to cancel the experiment after six days, even though it had been planned to last for two weeks.

By contrast with Milgram's experiments, which used the authoritative figure of an experimenter to prod cruel behavior, in Zimbardo's experiment there was no powerful authority demanding obedience and instructing participants to behave inhumanely. On the contrary, it seemed that the mere opportunity to wield power was sufficient to cause inhumane behavior.

Zimbardo argued forcefully that social roles and environmental conditions can bring out devastatingly cruel behavior. Taking his findings to the mainstream media, and even to congressional hearings on prison conditions, Zimbardo theorized that we can all too easily assume the roles we are given, letting them merge with our identities and give us permission to act in extreme ways. Power can be irresistible, and it can seemingly bring out bad behavior as easily as good.

Zimbardo's findings also say something about group dynamics. It's hard to imagine that the conflict would have escalated so dramatically if the experiment had involved just one guard and one prisoner. But pitting group versus group appeared to increase the severity of the conflict and the immoral behavior, in several ways. It was probably easier for any individual guard to justify his behavior when he could observe other guards doing the same things. And the fact that the prisoners were identified only by their assigned numbers, not by their names, probably encouraged the perception that they were an amorphous blob of objects, not individual human beings. They were conceptualized as a threat that needed to be controlled, not as individuals with thoughts, experiences, and emotions.

As reports of the experiment's results ignited the public conscience, Zimbardo's name recognition grew significantly. He used this platform to make his psychological findings more accessible to the public, and he encouraged the field of social psychology to take more interest in applying the results of its scientific work to the world at large. Zimbardo himself has shown interest not only in the applicability of his results to societal issues but also in the public's ability to have access to the education that experimental results can provide.

More recently, Zimbardo, relying in part on theories developed by other social psychologists, has summarized what he believes to be the seven forces that make the descent into evil behavior more likely:

» Mindless taking of the first small step
» Dehumanization of others
» Anonymity/deindividuation of the self
» Diffusion of personal responsibility
» Blind obedience to authority
» Uncritical conformity to group norms
» Passive tolerance of evil through inaction or indifference

THEN WHAT?

Zimbardo's findings have been used in many political and legal arenas, including the prison reform movement, as well as in the study of modern examples of extreme and cruel behavior, such as the torture of prisoners at Abu Ghraib. He has also used his findings to support antibullying education and initiatives. His additional work in social psychology has led to further study of shyness, for which he established

KEY EXPERIMENT The 1971 Stanford Prison Experiment involved 24 male undergraduates at Stanford University. Each of them had been screened and selected for stable emotional traits. Thus the participants were not likely to be hotheads or people overly sensitive to stressful situations, though it is worth noting that they all responded to a newspaper advertisement asking for participants in a study of prison life, which has been suggested by critics to mean that they were not a randomized, typical group to begin with.

The students were randomly assigned to be either prisoners or guards for the duration of the experiment. Of course, random assignment was key because it all but assured that there would be no meaningful, systematic differences in personality between the prisoners and the guards at the start of the experiment.

Though they had all, of course, agreed in advance to participate in the experiment, the actual booking of those who were to become prisoners was sprung on them as a surprise, and it was performed by members of the Palo Alto police department. Processing of the prisoners was conducted very much as in real life, with fingerprinting, mug shots, and rap sheets as well as actual jail cells. The prisoners were then transferred to a mock prison in the basement of Stanford's psychology department. At any given time, there were nine prisoners and nine guards (some of the participants were alternates).

Soon after their arrival, the prisoners, identified solely by number, were put into garments resembling dresses, with no undergarments, and were made to wear something akin to a hairnet. The guards, who wore dark sunglasses and carried sticks, were given few specific instructions for handling the prisoners other than being told that they were to keep order and that corporal punishment was not allowed. At first the mood was somewhat light, with the prisoners mocking the guards. But several of the guards soon grew frighteningly

a treatment clinic, and his most recent research has looked at the differences in how individuals perceive the passage of time and at how those perceptions affect the way time is used.

WHAT ABOUT ME?

When even randomly assigned power is liable to be so extremely abused, it is not hard to imagine how certain roles in real life—which are not random, and which we think we actually deserve to play—can power-hungry, commanding the prisoners to do repeated push-ups and deny-ing trips to the bathroom. They even sprayed fire extinguishers to break up a prisoner rebellion that arose as early as the second day, and extra guards, in the person of alternates, had to come in because of the uprising and the result-ing escalation on both sides.

Before long, some guards began stripping prisoners naked and imposing solitary confinement for longer than they were supposed to. Their behavior became frankly and increasingly sadistic, but it did nothing to unite the pris-oners, who began to turn on each other. The prisoners became more and more depressed and less and less autonomous, and the guards became more and more hostile. Zimbardo finally stopped the experiment, even though it offi-cially still had eight days to go.

Zimbardo himself served as superintendent of the prison, and another researcher with the experiment served as prison warden. These arrangements have generated some controversy, and there are different ways to view them. Critics say that because Zimbardo was not an unbiased observer, he probably created certain expectations for how people were supposed to behave, as he had a vested interest in seeing things spin somewhat out of control so as to prove just how dehumanizing the conditions in a prison can become. Perhaps this led to a sense of performing among some of the guards. Zimbardo himself has said that his role actually helped, scarily, underscore the results of the experiment itself—he got sucked in like all the rest, and perhaps he let the experiment go on too long because he was failing to view the participants as real people in distress and was dehumanizing them because of his desire to see the research go on. "I lost my sense of compassion," he has said. "I totally lost that."

provide justification for our poor treat-ment of others. Do you know anyone who treats restaurant servers like underlings? If you have such a friend, chances are that he or she is not rotten to the core and has some redeeming qualities; otherwise you probably wouldn't go out to dinner together. But something inherent in the social role of being served causes this person to lose a bit of his or her compas-sion and sense of fellowship.

As we've seen, anonymity can also con-tribute to problematic behavior. Why, for example, are online comment forums such

cesspools of hatred? There is evidence that the veil of anonymity encourages people to act more callously than they would if they were identified by name. Or maybe you've been the recipient of an anonymous, passive-aggressive note in your workplace, one with a derisive tone that you wouldn't have guessed could come from any of your coworkers. And have you ever seen a public restroom stall that was absolutely covered in graffiti? Maybe you even added to the mix—other people were there first, so you didn't feel fully responsible for what you did personally to deface the stall.

It is worth noting that even the criticisms leveled at Zimbardo's methodology—that his presence in the prison created expectations for the guards to perform; that the participants' self-selection may have meant that those who became guards already had too much interest in prison dynamics and were perhaps power-hungry—actually support the idea that what goes on in real-life prisons can be harrowing and horrifying. The guards in those facilities are self-selected, too, and it's reasonable to assume that at least some of them would like to become acquainted with what it feels like to have ultimate power over others. Guards in actual prisons may also be constantly observed and supervised by others who have an order-above-all-else mentality. So, from a methodological standpoint, Zimbardo's prison experiment may not have been as unbiased as it could have been, and the behaviors that emerged may not have done so in a pure way. But this actually strengthens the argument that what is going on in real prisons, where conditions are less randomized, is even worse.

So perhaps it's not absolutely true that any given person can turn sadistic in the right circumstances. But it likely is true, heartbreakingly so, that the right circumstances exist in very numerous and extreme ways outside the laboratory. And the people who have chosen to put themselves in those circumstances may be particularly prone to sadistic behavior.

Structuralism

Structuralism involves breaking down psychological experiences—thoughts, feelings, and behavior—into their most fundamental components and then exploring how these components connect to create more complex systems and phenomena. It posits that consciousness can be categorized in terms of basic elements, just as physical objects can be reduced to smaller parts. Wilhelm Wundt is often considered to have been the founder of this school of thought, and he is said to have been the first to call himself a psychologist; Edward B. Titchener was structuralism's primary torchbearer. Wundt's establishment of the first experimental psychology lab in 1879 led to decades of exploration that focused on defining and categorizing elements of the psychological experience. Structuralists were most interested in further understanding thoughts, emotions, and perception; they did not concern themselves as much with personality or behavior. Structuralism asserts that the main method of identifying fundamental components of psychological phenomena is introspection, an approach by which the structuralists intended to create descriptions of mental processes in the most basic terms. The term *introspection*, though it sounds like something you do on your day off while lying on the couch and wondering where your life is headed, refers in this case to a more scientific and structured exploration. A person, often a psychological theorist, would embark on the methodological observation of his or her own inner thought process under carefully controlled experimental conditions and would then report back as objectively as possible. Though empirically oriented, this method eventually fell out of favor as a research technique, given the question of how externally observable an individual's thoughts can be as well as possible biases and the impossibility of quantifying any given person's self-report. For this reason, structuralism also fell out of favor in psychology when psychology's focus shifted to more outwardly measurable mental processes and actions.

Functionalism

As its name implies, functionalism is concerned with what things *do*, and with the results that follow, rather than with what things *are*. It is the yin to the yang of structuralism, and it came into being as a reaction against structuralism. From the functionalist perspective, a psychological state's meaning emerges not from its components but from its end product. A functionalist would say that any mental state—sadness, ecstasy, guilt, boredom—is definable primarily by how it spurs subsequent action or mental states. In that sense, a functionalist would argue that different emotions that have led to the same reactions or behavior may not be so different after all. Moreover, from the functionalist perspective, that similarity of reactions or behavior is much more important than any differences in the mental states that gave rise to them. Given this focus on the actionable results of mental states, functionalism is more concerned than structuralism is with behavior, because functionalism emphasizes how a person's mental states will play out in the surrounding world. Functionalism, focusing less on mental processes than on the capabilities of the mind itself, places importance on experimental results that can be applied in practical ways, and so a lot of theorists under the functionalist umbrella have emphasized quantifiable, observable research results. Some of the earliest formal psychology laboratories were established by functionalists. Later functionalists, such as Edward Thorndike, can be viewed as early behaviorists, since they were most interested in the way that an organism responds and adapts to its environment.

Psychoanalysis

P sychoanalysis, more than any other school of thought, emphasizes the unconscious mind (sometimes called the *subconscious mind*, although the latter term is no longer scientifically acceptable). The purpose of psycho- analysis—the classic process that involves a patient's meeting routinely with a psychoanalyst, often while reclining on a couch and talking freely with the analyst, but without making eye contact—is to bring the patient's unconscious thoughts and feelings into conscious understanding so that the patient can gain insight into how these thoughts and feelings have affected his or her actions. Psychoanalysis explores how urges, desires, attitudes, and the old wounds that we don't acknowledge, even to ourselves, drive our personalities and our most fundamental patterns of behavior. Truthfully, many of the urges that psychoanalysis is most concerned with can be seen as very dark, and psycho- analysis can be viewed as portraying us as somewhat animalistic in our desires, and as driven strongly by lust, greed, and aggression. Psychoanalysis focuses not so much on relieving our immediate symptoms as on helping us gain clarity about past forces that have made us who we are, forces that are sometimes revealed in our dreams and even in the errors we make when we speak or write. Free association—responding with the very first thing that comes to mind when we hear a certain word—can also illuminate our unconscious thoughts and feelings. As a therapeutic tool, psychoanalysis has grown less popular over the years, eclipsed by other techniques (such as cognitive behavioral ther- apy) that focus more on the here and now. But psychoanalysis's vast influence remains, not just in the particularly pretty chaise longues that universally symbolize mental health treatment but also in the very real idea that even things we're not immediately aware of can affect our behavior in profound ways, and that we carry with us the scars and emo- tions of our childhood relationships.

Behaviorism

When you think of behaviorism, you may picture rats in mazes, or even the notorious Skinner box. If so, you're on the right track. Behaviorists believe that how we act is almost exclusively influenced by how we are conditioned; in other words, our behavior is overwhelmingly a response to the stimuli we encounter in our environment. Adherents of this school would also say that every experience we have, by either rewarding us or punishing us, serves to reinforce a certain behavior in the future. And sometimes the reward, or especially the punishment, comes about so automatically that we don't even realize it or can't control it. For example, imagine how you flinch when you see someone bring a pin near a balloon. You've been startled by that loud popping noise in the past, and your body has taught you to brace for it. Behaviorism also brought forth a new emphasis on quantitative measurement. Unlike some of the more subjective schools of thought that came before, behaviorism has been far more interested in quantifying than in conceptualizing. A typical behaviorist experiment has a lot in common with an experiment in physics or chemistry—it focuses on observable actions and reactions, and it looks to measure them in mathematical and systematic ways. For a behaviorist, the path to understanding is not introspection or interpretation. Behaviorism, to its credit, helped usher psychology into the world of the hard sciences and empirical validation.

Humanism

I f you get too bogged down in psychoanalysis or behaviorism, things can start to get a little . . . bleak. Either you're just an animal whose life purpose is driven by inescapable base urges or you're more like a machine—and not in a good way.

For many in the mid-20th century, those alternatives just didn't feel right. Don't humans have something bigger to offer? What about the quest to become a better person—to write, draw, laugh, connect, create music? And can't altruism exist for a reason other than its ability to make us feel good about ourselves? Enter the humanists. As a psychological school of thought, humanistic psychology, sometimes called the *third force* (after psychoanalysis and behaviorism), focuses on individual, positive growth rather than on the negative aspects and past baggage of the self. Its influence remains strong today—concepts dealing with emotional intelligence, connection, empathy, purpose, and meaning all fit very nicely into the humanistic framework. Humanistic psychology has also led to a much more connected, supportive vibe between patient and therapist. (In fact, the term *patient* is now often replaced by the term *client*.) Equality between therapist and client, demystification of the therapeutic process, and a more collaborative approach to the therapeutic work have been major thrusts of humanistic therapy. Group therapy also emerged from this framework.

Gestalt Psychology

Have you ever seen a particularly good optical illusion, perhaps a picture that looked at first glance like a vase but then became the profile of two people, and your brain couldn't decide which image to see? If there's really supposed to be a one-to-one correlation between our mental representations of objects in the external world and the objects themselves, then you might ask why we can even have optical illusions. Gestalt psychology is concerned with just that question—how we perceive the whole of an object, not just the discrete parts of which it's composed. Gestalt psychology can also be viewed as yet another departure from structuralism, since Gestalt psychologists emphasize that when things are broken down into excessively small components, something meaningful is lost. (The term *Gestalt* cannot be translated perfectly from German to English, but its general meaning is that of a configuration or a pattern of interrelated ideas.) In this way, Gestalt psychology is conceptually related to humanistic therapy, as evidenced in notions like self-actualization, which propose that essential components can build on each other in the creation of something that is qualitatively different—and, many would say, greater—than the sum of the constituent parts. Most of all, Gestalt psychology is concerned with our efforts to organize aspects of the world in personally meaningful ways. By contrast with behaviorism, Gestalt psychology posits that we place our greatest focus on our perceptions. Gestalt therapy, developed by Fritz Perls in the 1940s, is not precisely aligned with the concepts of Gestalt psychology, but it does focus on the parts that we play in our relationships with others, and on how our relationships affect our emotions in the present. Gestalt therapy is known for using a variety of role-playing techniques, including having the patient (or client) imagine that an empty chair holds a person with whom an issue needs to be worked through.

A Brief Survey of Abnormal Psychology

Abnormal is such a loaded word—and yet what, exactly, is normal? When we determine that a psychological disorder is present, we are using the word *abnormal* in a way that goes beyond its meaning of "strange" or "unusual." In clinical usage, the term *abnormal* represents three components:

» Some sort of psychological dysfunction

» Impairment or distress caused by the dysfunction

» The dysfunction's departure from what is culturally typical in the society to which the affected person belongs

Let's take the criterion of dysfunction first. The presence of a dysfunction simply indicates that, psychologically, something is not right. Maybe you're unable to feel pleasure, or you're seeing things that aren't there, or you're unable to focus on any given task.

Second, let's look at impairment or distress. Because of your psychological dysfunction, maybe you've been fired from your job, or your family relationships are deteriorating, or you're putting yourself in physical danger.

Third, why do we note that the dysfunction is culturally atypical? We do that so we won't inadvertently pathologize entire groups of people who engage in practices that seem odd to Western sensibilities but that are not necessarily unhealthy. For example, there may be people in your community who speak in tongues during their Pentecostal church services, and that behavior is culturally typical for them. But if you come from generations of straitlaced Episcopalians and suddenly start speaking in tongues, this startling new behavior won't be considered culturally typical for you.

The definitive roster of psychological disorders is housed in what's called the *Diagnostic and Statistical Manual of Mental Disorders*, abbreviated *DSM* and followed by a number indicating the edition of the manual. The current version is the *DSM-5*, which came out in 2013. There are more than 150 disorders included in the 20 chapters of the *DSM-5*. Here, some of the most prevalent conditions are described, with a focus on seven categories and the most common disorders within them.

Psychological and psychiatric treatment is beyond the scope of this book, of course, but if you recognize yourself in any of the following descriptions, please know that there is help. Treatments and prognoses vary—cognitive behavioral therapy, medication, interpersonal therapy, family therapy, and 12-step programs as well as other support groups may all have a role—but there are trained and licensed professionals who specialize in each of the disorders described here. Now more than ever, with rates of particular disorders skyrocketing, it's up to us to look out for ourselves and each other, and to seek help when we need it.

Mood Disorders

DEPRESSION

US prevalence 7 percent among adults

Major depressive disorder, or a major depressive episode, is far more complicated than just feeling sad. This is the most common psychological disorder, and people who suffer from it often experience changes in eating or sleeping patterns, feelings of hopelessness or worthlessness, difficulty concentrating and making decisions, and lack of motivation. Most classic for depressed people is the experience of *anhedonia*, which is a loss of pleasure or the inability to be excited by things that used to be of interest. Depressed people may isolate themselves socially and have negative thoughts about themselves. Sometimes they can also be anxious and irritable (depression can cause anxiety, and anxiety can lead to depression), or they may experience an uptick in substance abuse. Depression can be dangerous if left untreated. It carries a particularly significant suicide risk when it's severe and accompanied by feelings of hopelessness, recurrent thoughts of death, severe guilt and shame, and a sense that one is a burden to others.

BIPOLAR DISORDER

US prevalence 0.6 percent among adults

Whereas major depression involves just one pole of the emotional spectrum (a low mood), bipolar disorder involves both poles (mania or depression), and so it's sometimes also called *manic depression*. Mania is a severely elevated mood that often manifests in hyperenergetic activity, grandiose plans, and a general fast-and-loud pattern of bursting through life. It typically lasts a week or more and can come on suddenly. Its main danger comes from the increased impulsivity and risk taking that are often part of the package. People in the throes of a manic episode may feel wonderful, brimming with life and ideas, and they may also be agitated and prone to fights and aggressiveness. They may max out their credit cards with spontaneous entrepreneurial schemes or quit their jobs to travel, with no planning. Both sets of characteristics are brought on by the fact that the central nervous system is in overdrive; a manic episode is not set in motion by external factors like a relationship slight, nor is a manic episode indicated merely by hour-to-hour emotional shifts (this is why it's grossly inaccurate to describe your boss as bipolar merely because she was happy with you yesterday but is unhappy with you today). It is rare to experience a manic episode without a subsequent crash into depression, which can also pose a danger in terms of suicide risk. There are variations of the bipolar diagnosis, with bipolar I including full mania and full depression and bipolar II indicating full depression but with manic episodes that are not as severe (less severe mania, which is not a disorder in itself, is often referred to as *hypomania*).

SEASONAL AFFECTIVE DISORDER

US prevalence Varies widely with latitude, increasing at higher latitudes

In seasonal affective disorder (SAD), a subtype of major depression, moods follow a seasonal pattern. In a typical case of SAD, a person feels depressed over the course of the winter, but his or her mood elevates, perhaps even to the point of resembling mania or hypomania, in the spring. While many of us might get some winter doldrums or feel stressed or lonely during the winter holidays, SAD appears to be more biologically triggered and probably has to do not with changes in temperature but rather with changes in daylight that restrict the amount of naturally available ultraviolet light. This is why people affected by SAD may be particularly helped by physiological interventions like the use of a lightbox in the winter, to gain exposure to certain frequencies of light and that can help elevate mood.

PERIPARTUM DEPRESSION

US prevalence 3 to 6 percent of women who have recently given birth

Like the term *seasonal affective disorder*, the term *peripartum depression* technically specifies a major depressive episode, and it's important to note that this diagnosis includes not just women who have recently given birth (and who are therefore suffering from *postpartum depression*) but also women who are pregnant. There may very well be a biological predisposition to peripartum depression, especially among women who had a history of depression before becoming pregnant. Psychotic symptoms—involving hallucinations and delusions, often related to the baby—can be present in particularly severe cases. Interestingly enough, nonbiological parents and biological fathers may also be prone to similar mood shifts around the experience of having a new child, since the child's arrival may be accompanied by emotional upheavals and lifestyle disruptions as well as by mood disturbances and by hormonal changes occurring in response to time spent with the child (new fathers show a drop in testosterone early in the baby's life).

Anxiety Disorders

PANIC DISORDER

US prevalence 2.5 percent among adults

Someone who suffers from panic disorder (as opposed to specific phobias) has unexpected panic attacks. There is no particular known trigger, which makes the attacks feel even more scarily out of the person's control, to the point where a panic attack itself becomes something to be afraid of. Perhaps the person fears the results of the attack and the embarrassment or safety implications that it will have: *What if I have a panic attack in the middle of a board meeting or while driving on the freeway?* Or maybe the person worries that a panic attack will endanger physical well-being, cause a loss of control, or lead to actually going crazy. A panic attack involves a series of physiological and psychological symptoms that come on rather abruptly and are felt for what is usually a brief period—most panic attacks subside after 15 minutes or so—but the experience is intensely negative in spite of its brevity. Anyone who has had a panic attack can pinpoint the starting and end points pretty well—it is not a diffuse feeling. Heart palpitations, nausea, shortness of breath, dizziness, trembling, hot flashes, a sense of going crazy, a fear of dying, and a sense of being outside oneself are among the most common symptoms of a panic attack. Keep in mind that a person can also feel some of the same physical symptoms during pleasurable activity, such as riding a roller coaster or getting a good workout. It is the context of the symptoms that matters. In a panic attack, the feelings are intensely negative and unwanted, and in panic disorder, they lead to daily fear of their recurrence.

SPECIFIC PHOBIAS

US prevalence 8 percent among adults

Specific phobias—for example, those involving fear of animals or insects, of the natural environment (storms; open water), and of particular locations (small or crowded spaces; airplanes), and those involving fear of blood, injury, and injections (the latter group seems to have a strong genetic basis)—are among the most straightforward and easily treatable psychological disorders. As its name suggests, a specific phobia involves recurrent panic attacks triggered by a specific situation or object. These panic attacks usually lead to avoidance of the trigger, to the point where the avoidant behavior gets in the way of everyday life. The panic is out of proportion to any actual danger presented by the trigger, and when the phobia is severe enough, even hearing the name or seeing a picture of the feared object or situation can lead to anxiety.

SOCIAL ANXIETY DISORDER

US prevalence 7 percent among adults

This disorder is not the same thing as being introverted, and it's more extreme than being shy. Having social anxiety disorder means having the experience of distress and debilitating anxiety in a social situation. It could be public speaking or small talk or (for some people with a specific subtype) a performance situation like participating in a sport or playing music. Social anxiety can often turn into a full-fledged panic attack, and the idea of being negatively evaluated fuels the fire. People with social anxiety disorder would love to feel normal in social interactions and not have to avoid them (or endure them with such great distress), but negative thoughts and physical anxiety create a cycle of fear and apprehension that gets in the way of their experiencing life as they want to.

GENERALIZED ANXIETY DISORDER

US prevalence 2.9 percent among adults

Unlike the previously mentioned anxiety disorders, people with generalized anxiety disorder (GAD) might not experience any panic attacks at all. But their overall level of anxiety is always high, and their worries encompass not just dogs or parties or having a panic attack but several different areas of their lives. People with GAD are also affected in a physical way, often experiencing sleep problems, chronic muscle tension, and—though this seems counterintuitive—fatigue (since their bodies and minds are constantly on high alert). They find it very difficult to control or contain their worry, and it starts to have an abnormally significant impact on their daily lives.

Obsessive-Compulsive and Related Disorders

OBSESSIVE-COMPULSIVE DISORDER

US prevalence 1.2 percent among adults

Obsessive-compulsive disorder (OCD) is greatly misunderstood. Suffering from OCD does not mean being overly organized or anal. Rather, its sufferers are plagued by intrusive, disturbing thoughts (obsessions), and by compelling urges or repetitive rituals (compulsions), by which they try to reduce the distress that their disturbing thoughts bring on. Their compulsions don't typically resolve their anxiety very well, and so a person with OCD is often trapped in a seemingly endless loop of bothersome obsessions that lead to compulsions that in turn take up a lot of time and energy. Common obsessions involve such areas as concerns over hygiene, fear of something bad happening, a need for symmetry, aggressive urges, or fear of losing control. Common compulsions often, but not always, correspond to particular obsessions—washing to relieve a hygiene obsession, checking locks and appliances to relieve fear of a burglary or a fire, ordering and arranging objects to satisfy a need for symmetry. Counting is another common compulsion, and physical tics can develop as well. The most fundamental part of OCD is *thought-action fusion*, or behavior reflecting the belief that thoughts are dangerous in their own right. The more a person with OCD tries to fight an obsessive thought, the more bothersome and persistent it becomes. People who suffer from OCD can be locked in constant battle with thoughts that people without OCD will often just experience and then let go.

HOARDING DISORDER

US prevalence 4 percent among adults

Suffering from hoarding disorder—which is no longer categorized as a subtype of obsessive-compulsive disorder but is instead now seen as a disorder in its own right—means more than just being a packrat or having substantial collections of specific items. People with hoarding disorder find it very difficult or impossible to part with everyday objects, and they accumulate them to such an extent that they create living conditions hazardous to their own health and safety and to that of the people who live with them. Those with hoarding disorder sometimes have insight into the nature of their obsession with keeping items but are often resistant to seeing just how extreme their behavior has become. Their obsessional emotional attachment to items, and their high anxiety about what will happen if they get rid of them, typically causes major problems with emotional functioning and can destroy relationships.

BODY DYSMORPHIC DISORDER

US prevalence 2.4 percent among adults

Individuals with body dysmorphic disorder experience significant unrest over what they perceive to be flaws in their appearance, and they are preoccupied with one or many areas of their bodies that they see as abnormal or ugly. Their concerns are grossly exaggerated; any objective abnormality in their appearance, if indeed it exists, is typically not nearly as extreme as they believe it to be. The time and the mental energy they expend in worry about their alleged flaws can take over their lives, and people with this disorder often develop compulsive types of behavior as they try to relieve their distress (for example, they may repeatedly check mirrors, purchase various beauty projects, or seek out plastic surgery). Their insight into their distorted perceptions can vary. Some people recognize that their preoccupations are out of proportion to their actual appearance, and others border on delusional thinking, given how certain they are about the extreme negativity of their appearance.

Trauma- and Stressor- Related Disorders

POST-TRAUMATIC STRESS DISORDER

US prevalence 3.5 percent among adults

Post-traumatic stress disorder (PTSD) involves not just the experience of a trauma but also serious challenges and disruptions to daily life in the trauma's aftermath. A *trauma* is defined as an experience of great helplessness and horror, often accompanied by feeling one's life is in danger, or as the direct witnessing of such an experience suffered by another. Although a trauma— experiencing sexual assault, a car accident, or military combat—is the first component of PTSD, not everyone who suffers a trauma will develop the disorder. But those who do will start to see significant impairment in daily life, sometimes months or even years after the trauma. Their symptoms include chronic flashbacks and nightmares, avoidance of anything that reminds them of the trauma, emotional numbness, and hypervigilance (for example, startling very easily). A person's life becomes defined by the trauma, with the whole personality likely undergoing changes, and behavior—even if in the form of denial or avoidance of talking about the trauma—is drastically altered compared to what it was before the traumatic experience.

ADJUSTMENT DISORDERS

US prevalence 5 to 20 percent among adults in outpatient mental health treatment

Adjustment disorders belong to the category of disorders that encompasses reactions to clear-cut stressors. These disorders are very common among people who seek mental health treatment, especially when people have trouble coping with an actual life disturbance, as opposed to exhibiting symptoms that are aligned with specific psychological disorders. Such disturbances include relationship breakups, being fired from a job, and many other stressors. For adjustment disorder diagnosis, the stressor must have occurred within the past three months, and the distress (which can vary in presentation) must hinder day-to-day functioning or be out of proportion to the actual stressor. Naturally, adjustment disorder would not be diagnosed when another psychological disorder (such as a major depressive episode) is a better fit for the circumstances, nor during a typical grieving process. The diagnosis of adjustment disorder can be specified as including a depressed mood, anxiety, or both, in addition to behavioral problems and physical difficulties like insomnia and indigestion.

Neurodevelopmental Disorders

ATTENTION DEFICIT/ HYPERACTIVITY DISORDER

US prevalence 5 percent among children; 2.5 percent among adults

Attention deficit/hyperactivity disorder (ADHD) encompasses two main clusters of challenges. The first involves an overly high level of distractibility, with inability to focus and concentrate, and the second is physical overactivity, usually manifesting as hyperactivity and inability to sit still and often accompanied by impulsivity. Also associated with ADHD are forgetfulness, disorganization, inability to follow through with tasks, and inability to wait for one's turn to speak or act. Sometimes adults are diagnosed only with attention deficit disorder (ADD) rather than with ADHD, since their childhood hyperactivity has worked its way out of their systems. No matter when ADHD is diagnosed, there has to be evidence that the symptoms existed in childhood, before age 12. This is an important (if often ignored) criterion, since ADHD is a developmental disorder, which means that the brain of a person with the disorder has a way of processing things that is qualitatively different from the way things are processed by the brain

of someone who doesn't suffer from the disorder. ADHD is not something that develops suddenly, in the wake of stress or lifestyle changes, but stress and lifestyle changes can certainly cause symptoms that mimic ADHD, as can depression, anxiety, and conduct problems.

AUTISM SPECTRUM DISORDER

US prevalence 1 percent among adults and children

The main symptomology of autism spectrum disorder involves atypical or ritualized behavior as well as deficits in communication skills and social skills. (Having autism disorder is often referred to as being "on the spectrum.") Autism is not a one-size-fits-all diagnosis, and it encompasses a large range of gradations of functioning. In fact, there are few other disorders in which variance is so great. Some children on the spectrum have never so much as made eye contact with their parents, whereas others grow up to be engineers or professors whose difficulties appear mainly in social interactions. Asperger's disorder, formerly listed in the *DSM* as a disorder in its own right, is now categorized as falling on the autism spectrum, although Asperger's disorder can still be diagnosed by physicians and others who use a classification system other than the *DSM-5*. Asperger's disorder is essentially high-functioning autism, with the main challenges being social in nature. It is not shyness and does not come from a place of anxiety; rather, it's indicated by lack of interest in social interaction and by the inability to interact in social settings in typical ways. As is true of the autism spectrum in general, in Asperger's disorder there is frequently an inability to process other people's emotional experience. Children on the autism spectrum show unusual repetitive behaviors, such as arm flapping, lining up toys over and over again, rocking, or even slapping themselves. Such actions, which appear over and over again, typically don't seem to serve an outward purpose, but they probably serve a self-soothing or even self-stimulating function for the child. Also in this category of behavior is a tunnel-like restriction of interests, one that can look obsessive. Some children on the autism spectrum may be particularly sensitive to sensory stimuli like heat, light, and noise and even to the texture of clothing, and they may have severe difficulty with changes in routine or with times of transition throughout the day.

Psychotic Disorders

SCHIZOPHRENIA

US prevalence 0.5 percent among adults

Schizophrenia is widely misunderstood. Often confused with dissociative identity disorder (the experience of having multiple personalities), and mistakenly seen as presenting an increased risk of violence, schizophrenia is a serious disorder that entails psychotic symptoms and a significant mental break from reality. Though the word *psychotic* is often tossed about in American slang, it actually describes the experience of either delusions (beliefs that are out of touch with reality) or hallucinations (sensory experiences that are altered or distorted). Hallucinations can involve any of the five senses, but people with schizophrenia most commonly have auditory hallucinations, such as hearing voices. Having delusions goes beyond simply having an unorthodox set of beliefs (as in holding to a simple conspiracy theory); delusions are more systematic and indicate truly disordered thought patterns. Sometimes the difference between being psychotic and believing in a conspiracy theory can be a matter of controversy, but surely there is a difference between believing that the government has secret surveillance systems in place and believing that the government has implanted a microchip in every citizen's brain. Schizophrenia may include a relatively sudden psychotic break, which often happens in the late teens or early twenties. The term *positive symptoms* is used for the presence of experiences (chiefly hallucinations and delusions) that have no objective basis in reality. The term *negative symptoms* is used for the absence of phenomena (such as speech, social interaction, and emotional expression) that are normally present. Additional symptoms may include disorganized speech, inappropriate or flat emotional expression, and even catatonic bodily movements. Without adequate treatment, schizophrenia seriously impairs functioning, but it varies in its severity. Some people with schizophrenia are unable to care for themselves or to engage in any cohesive interaction with the world around them. Others are able to hang on to jobs and relationships while battling their delusions and hallucinations, and some of them do so to great acclaim, as did the mathematician John Forbes Nash Jr., whose story was told in the biography and film *A Beautiful Mind*, and Elyn Saks, a professor of law and psychology whose autobiography, *The Center Cannot Hold*, recounts her triumphant path through the experience of schizophrenia and its treatment.

Neurocognitive Disorders

MILD OR MAJOR NEUROCOGNITIVE IMPAIRMENT

US prevalence 1.5 percent among adults 65 years old; 30 percent among adults 85 years old

What used to be called *dementia* is now called *neurocognitive impairment*, and it can be diagnosed as mild or major, classifications that aid in the detection of early cases. Having neurocognitive impairment means exhibiting systematic and comprehensive cognitive deficits across memory, learning, and consciousness. Neurocognitive impairment has several possible causes, including long-term substance abuse, stroke, and various genetic syndromes. The most common cause is Alzheimer's disease, in which irreversible neurocognitive impairment tends to come on gradually, in someone's 60s or 70s. Eventually, all types of memory are affected, including autobiographical memory and muscle memory (it may become impossible for someone to remember how to turn a doorknob or use a comb, for instance). Difficulty recognizing faces or objects often manifests as well, as do increasing disorientation and confusion. Though neurocognitive impairment, by its nature, involves thought processes, emotional functioning and personality are often affected, too. Agitation, fear, and depression often accompany the diagnosis. Loved ones and caregivers may experience a high level of stress and heartbreak, so it's important to seek support for them as well.

CHRONIC TRAUMATIC ENCEPHALOPATHY

US prevalence As yet unclear among professional athletes in contact sports

Chronic traumatic encephalopathy (CTE) is a syndrome increasingly identified in athletes who have experienced years and years of hits to the head, even below the level of concussion. It is thought that long-term repetitive impacts on the brain create an accumulation of proteins that eventually cause symptoms resembling those of neurocognitive impairment. CTE can be definitively diagnosed only after autopsy, but it often strikes sooner than Alzheimer's disease and is associated with similar symptoms as well as with erratic behavior, delusional thinking, substance abuse, and heightened risk of suicide.

DELIRIUM

US prevalence 1.5 percent among adults 65 and older; prevalence rises with age as well as in care facilities

Though delirium sometimes overlaps with neurocognitive impairment, it may come on very suddenly, even without existing impairment. Fortunately, it may also abate on its own after a few days or weeks. It is common in older people who are experiencing a sudden change in environment, an uptick in stress, or increased immobility. All these factors tend to exist when someone has been hospitalized for a physical procedure or problem, and so delirium is quite common among elderly people in hospitals. Across age groups, delirium can also be brought on by infections, toxins, substance abuse, and medical conditions. In delirium, a person may suddenly become confused and disoriented, unable to recognize friends and family or to recall key information, with fluctuations in mental functioning. With proper support, and after the person has returned to a less stressful routine, delirium often reverses itself.

Substance-Related Disorders

ALCOHOL-USE DISORDER

US prevalence for alcohol-use disorder, the most common substance-related disorder: 8.5 percent among adults

Substance abuse and dependence are widespread problems, and it can sometimes be hard to know where the line is in terms of what is unhealthy. Substance-related disorders are characterized by their effects on the body, and the substances themselves fall into the categories of depressants, stimulants, opiates, and hallucinogens. Classic signs of substance *abuse* include letting a substance get in the way of relationships, work, school, or other responsibilities; using the substance when it's physically dangerous to do so; trying to cut back and being unable to do so; using the substance in increasingly large amounts, or for longer than intended; strong cravings for the substance; and spending quite a lot of time getting or using the substance. Substance *dependence*, synonymous with addiction, has physiological as well as psychological components. The physiological components include *tolerance* (an inability, over time, to get the same effects from ingesting the same amount of the substance) and *withdrawal symptoms* (distressing and uncomfortable physical and psychological sensations that come on when the body has to go without the substance). Unfortunately, tolerance and withdrawal symptoms can combine to keep a person trapped in an addictive cycle. The person may no longer be using the substance to get high but may need it to keep from experiencing withdrawal symptoms. The psychological components of substance dependence include overwhelming cravings as well as substance-seeking behavior that impairs daily functioning. These components may be present even when the substance is not necessarily known for being physically addictive (for example, someone may not be physically addicted to marijuana but spends every moment wondering how to get it, no longer cares to see friends, and spends every last dime on marijuana while neglecting to buy basic necessities). As it happens, the *DSM-5* no longer differentiates between substance abuse and substance dependence but now includes a model for diagnosing mild, moderate, or severe substance-related disorders. It is also worth noting that the *DSM-5* includes in this category one disorder that is not technically related to a chemical compound—gambling disorder—because the symptoms of compulsive gambling closely mimic those of substance abuse and substance dependence and even include tolerance and withdrawal.

Glossary

16PF Raymond Cattell's personality inventory, a self-report questionnaire that measures levels of 16 salient traits said to vary across individuals.

A-NOT-B ERROR (PERSEVERATIVE ERROR) In developmental psychology, as advanced by Jean Piaget, this error is committed by a baby 10 months old or younger who has witnessed an object being hidden in a particular place but nevertheless looks for the object in the last place he or she found it.

ACCOMMODATION In developmental psychology, as advanced by Jean Piaget, the adjustment or modification of a mental schema in order to fit new information gleaned from the environment.

ANIMA Carl Jung's term for the feminine personality archetype in the unconscious mind of a man.

ANIMUS Carl Jung's term for the masculine personality archetype in the unconscious mind of a woman.

APHASIA A language disorder that involves deficits in vocal expression.

APPROACH-APPROACH CONFLICT According to Kurt Lewin, the psychological process that occurs when someone has to decide between two desirable options.

APPROACH-AVOIDANCE CONFLICT According to Kurt Lewin, the psychological process that occurs when someone has to decide whether to choose an option that has both positive and negative qualities.

ARBITRARY INFERENCES Aaron Beck's term for irrational connections made between phenomena that are actually unrelated.

ARCHETYPE Carl Jung's term for one of a set of universal features within the collective unconscious.

ASSIMILATION In developmental psychology, as advanced by Jean Piaget, the incorporation of new information into an existing mental schema.

AVOIDANCE-AVOIDANCE CONFLICT For Kurt Lewin, the psychological process that occurs when someone has to choose between two undesirable options.

B-NEEDS In Abraham Maslow's hierarchy of needs, the "being" needs, which are never fully satisfied and encourage the drive toward self-actualization.

BASIC ANXIETY Karen Horney's term for the distress that children feel when the world seems scary and unpredictable to them.

BRAIN LOCALIZATION The idea that particular areas of the brain are responsible for specific cognitive processes, emotions, and types of behavior.

BROCA'S AREA The region of the brain's frontal lobe, in the dominant hemisphere, responsible for producing speech; named for Paul Broca, who first identified it.

CARDINAL TRAITS Gordon Allport's term for personality characteristics so dominant as to control behavior and significantly define a person.

CENTRAL TRAITS Gordon Allport's term for basic personality characteristics that are present, to various degrees, in almost everyone.

CLIENT-CENTERED PSYCHOTHERAPY As developed by Carl Rogers, a type of humanistic psychotherapy emphasizing warmth and collaboration between therapist and client, the therapist's unconditional positive regard of the client, and the client's potential for growth.

COGNITIVE DISSONANCE According to Leon Festinger, the distress that an individual feels when two inconsistent beliefs, feelings, or actions clash; cognitive dissonance prompts the individual to minimize unease by reinterpreting the situation in question.

COGNITIVE ERRORS Aaron Beck's term for a collection of irrationally held beliefs, such as those involved in overgeneralization or in dichotomous thinking, that often lead to depression or anxiety.

COGNITIVE THERAPY As developed by Aaron Beck and influenced by Albert Ellis, a psychotherapeutic framework focused on identifying and challenging automatic and maladaptive thoughts that influence emotions and behavior.

COLLECTIVE UNCONSCIOUS Carl Jung's term for universal thoughts and memories derived from human ancestors and existing within the psyche, outside conscious awareness.

CONCRETE OPERATIONAL Jean Piaget's term for the stage of cognitive development, typically between the ages of 7 and 11, when children can use logic but not yet abstraction to perform mental operations.

CONDITIONED STIMULUS In classical conditioning, as developed by Ivan Pavlov, a stimulus (such as the striking of a tuning fork) that has been paired enough times with an unconditioned stimulus (such as the presentation of meat powder) to evoke a response (such as salivation).

CONNECTIONISM Edward Thorndike's theory that learning is always the result of the connection between a stimulus and a response.

CONSERVATION OF QUANTITY The principle that quantity, such as mass or volume, stays constant for a substance even when the substance is put into different containers or forms; in developmental psychology, as advanced by Jean Piaget, a child's ability to automatically understand this principle does not appear until after the preoperational stage.

CONSTRUCTIVIST A term describing Jean Piaget's theory of learning, which states that individuals are active learners and build knowledge through their own specific experiences.

CRITICAL PERIODS OF DEVELOPMENT As hypothesized by the neurologist and linguist Eric Lenneberg, these periods are identified with certain age ranges within which particular skills or abilities (such as the ability to speak or write) are most readily acquired or must be acquired if they are to emerge at all.

CRYSTALLIZED INTELLIGENCE For Raymond Cattell, knowledge and experience derived over time, and the ability to use that knowledge in decision making.

CUPBOARD MODEL In psychoanalytic theory, the term for a particular conceptualization of mother-child bonding and attachment; according to this model, bonding takes place primarily because the mother meets her baby's biological needs.

DEEP STRUCTURE Noam Chomsky's term for the actual meaning of a sentence, regardless of the precise arrangement of the sentence's words (that is, its surface structure).

DEFENSE MECHANISMS In psychoanalytic theory, as developed by Sigmund Freud, dysfunctional mental or behavioral patterns intended to resolve the anxiety that arises when the desires of the id clash with the rules and expectations that have been absorbed by the superego.

DEINDIVIDUATION As reported by Philip Zimbardo in connection with the Stanford Prison Experiment, loss of the sense of self, thought to explain behavior that deviates from an individual's usual high moral standard.

DICHOTOMOUS THINKING A kind of binary thinking that construes situations in all-or-nothing or black-and-white terms; for Aaron Beck, a type of cognitive error likely to contribute to depression and anxiety.

D-NEEDS In Abraham Maslow's hierarchy of needs, the "deficiency" needs, which the individual is driven to meet, but which, once satisfied, are no longer motivating.

EGO In psychoanalytic theory, as developed by Sigmund Freud, the rational self that negotiates a balance between the id and the superego.

EPISODIC MEMORY Ulric Neisser's term for memory that is autobiographical in nature and directly related to personal experience.

EXCITATION The process of the brain's coming to alertness and becoming more highly attuned to its environment; this process plays a role in Hans Eysenck's personality theory.

EXISTENTIAL VACUUM For Viktor Frankl, the psychological void created when one perceives one's life to be meaningless.

EXPERIMENTAL NEUROSIS In classical conditioning, as developed by Ivan Pavlov, agitation in response to a requirement for excessive discrimination between gradations of the same conditioned stimulus (such as slight variations in pitch produced by the striking of a tuning fork).

EXTRAVERSION The tendency to be psychologically turned outward and to derive energy from the external environment and from other people.

FACE VALIDITY The degree to which the items included in an assessment appear to be appropriate for what they purport to measure, regardless of whether those items are in fact appropriate for that purpose.

FACTOR ANALYSIS A statistical procedure, often used in research on personality traits, that identifies clusters of covarying items; from a larger set of salient variables, factor analysis narrows down a smaller set.

FIELD THEORY Kurt Lewin's hypothesis that behavior is a function of an individual's characteristics and of his or her reactions to the environment.

FIXATION In psychoanalytic theory, as developed by Sigmund Freud, a permanent dysfunctional behavior or personality trait that originally developed because of a traumatic event or unmet needs during a particular psychosexual stage.

FIXED MINDSET According to Carol Dweck, a mental orientation aligned with the unwarranted belief that intelligence or abilities are unchangeable and cannot be significantly increased or improved through practice or effort.

FLASHBULB MEMORIES Ulric Neisser's term for memories of highly emotional and significant life moments, incidents often thought to be remembered vividly, although it has been shown that such memories are not necessarily accurate.

FLUID INTELLIGENCE For Raymond Cattell, the ability to use logic and strategy in solving novel problems.

FORMAL OPERATIONAL Jean Piaget's term for the stage of cognitive development, typically seen at the age of 12 and older, when children can use abstraction and hypothetical reasoning to perform higher mental operations.

FREUDIAN SLIP (SLIP OF THE TONGUE) Sigmund Freud's term for the unintentional substitution of one word for another, more socially appropriate word, revealing an unconscious feeling or motivation.

GAIN-LOSS THEORY OF ATTRACTION Elliot Aronson's hypothesis that one person will tend to like a second person more if the second person appears at first not to like the first person than if the second person likes the first person from the beginning.

GENETIC EPISTEMOLOGY Jean Piaget's term for his study of the origination of knowledge.

GROWTH MINDSET According to Carol Dweck, a mental orientation aligned with the belief that intelligence and abilities are malleable and can be increased or improved through practice, and that failure is an opportunity for learning.

HIERARCHY OF NEEDS Abraham Maslow's five-level conceptualization of the needs that motivate human behavior, ranging from those related to basic survival to those involved in self-actualization.

HIGHER-ORDER CONDITIONING In classical conditioning, as developed by Ivan Pavlov, the practice of using a conditioned stimulus (such as the striking of a tuning fork) in place of an unconditioned stimulus (such as the presentation of meat powder) as the basis of a new round of conditioning; second-order conditioning may be possible, but third-order conditioning probably is not.

HYPERINTENTION Viktor Frankl's term for the act of trying so hard to force some outcome that it cannot occur.

HYPERREFLECTION Viktor Frankl's term for the act of thinking so excessively about oneself or about something that the thinking becomes maladaptive.

ID In psychoanalytic theory, as developed by Sigmund Freud, the component of the unconscious mind that is the seat of animalistic urges, lust, and violence.

IDENTITY CRISIS Erik Erikson's term for the failure to achieve ego identity (that is, congruence between one's sense of self and one's actions) during adolescence.

ILLUSORY SUPERIORITY Stanley Milgram's term for the individual's erroneous self-assessment in comparing his or her skills, intelligence, or morality to the skills, intelligence, or morality of other people.

INFERIORITY COMPLEX Alfred Adler's term for a set of beliefs, emotions, and actions that represent an individual's attempt to overcome personal shortcomings, as the individual perceives them by comparing himself or herself with others.

INHIBITION The process of the brain's tuning out its environment and trying to lower its level of stimulation; this process plays a role in Hans Eysenck's personality theory.

INTERVAL SCHEDULE In operant conditioning, as developed by B. F. Skinner, a schedule of reinforcement wherein rewards are given for a particular type of behavior after a certain amount of time has elapsed, as opposed to being given after the behavior has been performed a certain number of times.

INTROVERSION The tendency to be psychologically turned inward and to derive energy from one's own thoughts and from being alone.

JAMES–LANGE THEORY OF EMOTION The theory that psychological experience is a function of physiological events (for example, if the heart beats faster and the hair stands on end, the emotion of fear is experienced as a result).

JIGSAW CLASSROOM As developed by Elliot Aronson, an educational approach wherein heterogeneous groups of students collaborate, with each student fulfilling a specific role; this approach has been shown to increase learning and motivation and to reduce conflict.

L DATA Raymond Cattell's term for the life record, or information collected from society about a person, such as peer evaluations and court data.

LANGUAGE ACQUISITION DEVICE (LAD) A part of the brain hypothesized by Noam Chomsky to be preprogrammed for learning language and to serve as a processor.

LAW OF DISUSE Edward Thorndike's statement of his theory that the less frequently a stimulus and a response are connected, the less ingrained their association (that is, learning) becomes.

LAW OF EFFECT Edward Thorndike's statement of his theory that behavior evoking a pleasurable response is more likely to be repeated than behavior evoking an unpleasant response.

LAW OF USE Edward Thorndike's statement of his theory that the more frequently a stimulus and a response are connected, the more ingrained their association (that is, learning) becomes.

LEADERSHIP CULTURE Kurt Lewin's term for the workplace environment, which he characterizes as democratic, authoritarian, or laissez-faire, according to the style set by organizational leaders.

LEARNING CURVE A term associated with Edward Thorndike's observation that performance follows a trajectory, improving with repeated practice and eventually reaching its peak, where it plateaus.

LEWIN'S EQUATION Kurt Lewin's more specific conceptualization of his field theory, the hypothesis that individual behavior is a function of personal psychological characteristics and of how those characteristics react to the individual's environment.

LIFE CRISES In Erik Erikson's theory of development, particular conflicts characteristic of eight distinct psychosocial stages that unfold consecutively over an individual's lifetime.

LIFE SPACE Kurt Lewin's term for the totality of the influences acting on an individual at any given time.

LOGOTHERAPY A type of psychotherapy developed by Viktor Frankl that emphasizes the search for purpose and meaning in life.

MASS NEUROTIC TRIAD In Viktor Frankl's logotherapy, the three forces of depression, agitation, and addiction, which result from lack of meaning in one's life or from misdirection in the search for meaning.

MENTAL SERIATION The mind's arrangement of items by degree, such as by size; in developmental psychology, as advanced by Jean Piaget, this capacity is thought to emerge during the concrete operational stage.

MICROGENETIC Lev Vygotsky's term to describe the types of small changes that occur in an individual's development over brief periods of time.

MIND-BODY PROBLEM The philosophical question, debated for centuries, about the nature of the mind and the body and their interaction with each other.

MISINFORMATION EFFECT Elizabeth Loftus's term for the development of a false recollection after inaccurate information has been absorbed by and stored in memory.

MODELING THERAPY As developed by Albert Bandura, a type of psychotherapy in which people overcome their fears and meet other challenges by watching others overcome the same fears and meet the same challenges.

MORPHEMES The smallest units of meaning that belong to a particular language; a morpheme may be an individual word but also a prefix, a suffix, or a word root that carries meaning.

MYERS-BRIGGS TYPE INDICATOR (MBTI) A personality inventory derived from the ideas of Carl Jung that measures traits along the four axes of extraversion/introversion, sensing/intuition, thinking/feeling, and judging/perceiving.

NATIVIST THEORY OF LANGUAGE ACQUISITION The theory, such as the one reflected in Noam Chomsky's hypothesis of the brain's language acquisition device (LAD), that humans are biologically preprogrammed to learn language.

NATURAL SELECTION In Charles Darwin's theory of evolution, nature's elimination, over time, of an organism's weaker traits so as to make the organism better adapted to its environment and increase the organism's chances of surviving long enough to produce offspring that will carry stronger, more adaptive traits and thus help ensure the continuation of the species to which the organism belongs.

NEUROSIS A phenomenon now generally called distress or agitation; in Karen Horney's theory, anxiety that continually accompanies the attempt to get by in day-to-day life.

NEUROTIC NEEDS In Karen Horney's theory, 10 extreme, all-encompassing emotional needs that represent maladaptive patterns arising from deficits in an individual's development, often in connection with the individual's parents.

OBJECT PERMANENCE The understanding, thought to solidify over the course of Jean Piaget's sensorimotor stage, that objects continue to exist even when they are outside immediate sensory awareness.

OEDIPUS COMPLEX In psychoanalytic theory, as developed by Sigmund Freud, the dilemma of the child who sexually desires the opposite-sex parent and wants to minimize competition by excluding the same-sex parent.

ONTOGENETIC Lev Vygotsky's term to describe the type of development (often the type of most interest to developmental psychologists) that occurs over the lifetime of an individual.

PARADOXICAL INTENTION As encouraged therapeutically by Viktor Frankl, a stance of actively wishing for something that has been feared or engaging in a fearful activity for the purpose of making that thing or that activity less likely to provoke anxiety in the future.

PERSEVERATIVE FUNCTIONAL AUTONOMY For Gordon Allport, an attribute of a habit that has persisted long after its original purpose was fulfilled.

PERSONA Carl Jung's term for the external role that someone plays in the world.

PHONEMES The smallest, most elemental units of sound that belong to a particular spoken language; roughly 40 phonemes exist in American English.

PHYLOGENETIC Lev Vygotsky's term to describe the type of development affected by thousands of years of evolutionary forces.

POVERTY-OF-STIMULUS ARGUMENT The assertion that children's continuous repetition of the spoken language they hear is not enough to account for their learning to speak meaningfully; this is Noam Chomsky's argument for why behavioral theories are insufficient to explain language development.

PRATFALL EFFECT Elliot Aronson's term for the discovery that individuals will tend to like a competent person more if the person makes a minor mistake than if the person performs perfectly.

PREOPERATIONAL Jean Piaget's term for the stage of development, thought to occur typically from about the age of 2 to the age of 7, when representational thought and language increase significantly but mental operations are still basic.

PRESENTING PROBLEM The issue that someone initially brings to a psychotherapist and describes as the challenge that drove the decision to seek therapy; this issue may or may not represent the true depth of what the individual is going through emotionally.

PROPRIATE FUNCTIONAL AUTONOMY For Gordon Allport, an attribute of behavior that reflects an individual's true self and aligns with his or her values.

PROPRIUM Gordon Allport's term for the individual's true self.

PSYCHOHISTORY A biographical narrative that includes exploration of its well-known subject's psychological characteristics; in 1970, Erik Erikson won a Pulitzer Prize for his psychohistory of Gandhi.

PSYCHOMETRICS The assessment and measurement of psychological phenomena like mood, memory, cognitive states, and personality.

PSYCHOSEXUAL STAGES In psychoanalytic theory, as developed by Sigmund Freud, periods that unfold universally throughout child development and entail a combination of biological and psychological maturation.

PUZZLE BOX An apparatus that Edward Thorndike used in many of his experiments on animal learning.

Q DATA Raymond Cattell's term for personality information gleaned from self-reports.

RATIO SCHEDULE In operant conditioning, as developed by B. F. Skinner, a schedule of reinforcement wherein rewards are given after a particular type of behavior has been performed a certain number of times, as opposed to being given after a certain amount of time has elapsed.

RATIONAL-EMOTIVE BEHAVIOR THERAPY (REBT) As developed by Albert Ellis, a type of psychotherapy that involves challenging one's irrational and dysfunctional thoughts and altering one's behavior accordingly; a forerunner to cognitive therapy.

REPISODIC MEMORY Ulric Neisser's term for inaccurate memory of events or experiences (a play on the term *episodic memory*).

SCHEDULES OF REINFORCEMENT In operant conditioning, as developed by B. F. Skinner, patterns of reward or punishment that, over time, determine behavior; different schedules produce different levels of intensity in their effects on behavior.

SCHEMAS (SCHEMATA) Mental groupings that an individual uses to organize and categorize information into meaningful patterns so as to better understand the world.

SECONDARY TRAITS Gordon Allport's term for personality characteristics that arise only in certain contexts or situations.

SELF Carl Jung's term for the overarching archetype that unifies the individual's conscious and unconscious minds.

SELF-ACTUALIZATION In Abraham Maslow's hierarchy of needs, the final and highest need, concerned with the drive to fulfill one's abilities and live a purposeful and fully engaged life; only a minority of people reach this level.

SELF-CONTROL THERAPY As developed by Albert Bandura, a type of psychotherapy concerned with overcoming habits through observation of one's behavior and alteration of one's environment.

SELF-EFFICACY For Albert Bandura, the effect of a person's belief in his or her ability to perform a certain task.

SELF-SERVING BIAS For Raymond Cattell, the general desire to enhance one's positive attributes, increase one's self-esteem, or present oneself in a more favorable light; in self-reports of personality, this bias often leads to inaccurate assessments.

SEMANTIC MEMORY Ulric Neisser's term for memory of knowledge and information that has been learned and that is not directly related to personal experience.

SENSORIMOTOR Jean Piaget's term for the stage of cognitive development, typically between birth and the age of 2, when children's mental operations depend primarily on the interaction between their bodies and the environment.

SEXUAL SELECTION In Charles Darwin's evolutionary theory, an organism's seeking out of mates with traits deemed desirable for reproduction and thus more likely to help ensure the continuation of the species to which the organism belongs.

SHADOW Carl Jung's term for aspects of the personality that are inaccessible to conscious understanding.

SHAPING In operant conditioning, as developed by B. F. Skinner, the practice of giving reinforcement for behavior that approximates a desired type of behavior so as to eventually produce the desired behavior itself.

SOCIAL COMPARISON THEORY Leon Festinger's hypothesis that we assess ourselves and our abilities by continually measuring ourselves against others.

SOCIAL INTEREST Alfred Adler's term for a general concern directed toward others and toward one's relationships with them, and for the motivation to think of oneself as belonging to a larger community.

SOCIAL LEARNING THEORY Albert Bandura's theory that behavior is learned through modeling and imitation.

SOCIAL MODELING The part of Albert Bandura's social learning theory that deals with how people learn from others' behavior; its four components are attention, retention, reproduction, and motivation.

SOCIOCULTURAL A term describing Lev Vygotsky's theories of learning and cognitive development and referring specifically to his theories' focus on the dual influences of culture and social interactions.

SOCIOHISTORICAL In Lev Vygotsky's theories of learning and development, a term to describe cultural changes that have occurred over time and impacted how learning has taken place.

SOURCE TRAITS In Raymond Cattell's personality theory, a term for facets of personality that are fundamental to an individual.

STIMULUS GENERALIZATION In classical conditioning, as developed by Ivan Pavlov, an effect that can occur even though a conditioned stimulus (such as the striking of a tuning fork) is not always presented in the same way.

STREAM OF CONSCIOUSNESS Henry James's concept of conscious thoughts flowing continuously and inseparably; in later usage, the expression of a continuous chain of these thoughts.

SUNDAY NEUROSIS Viktor Frankl's term for the boredom and malaise that can set in during times of leisure and motivate superficial pleasures or the consumption of material goods.

SUPEREGO In psychoanalytic theory, as developed by Sigmund Freud, the component of the mind that has absorbed rules, values, and morals and that acts to guide behavior, often in opposition to the id.

SURFACE STRUCTURE Noam Chomsky's term for the precise arrangement of the words in a sentence, in contrast with the meaning of the sentence (that is, the sentence's deep structure); different sentences can have different surface structures but the same deep structure.

SURFACE TRAITS In Raymond Cattell's personality theory, a term for specific facets of personality that are not all-encompassing for an individual.

SYNCHRONICITY Carl Jung's term for the phenomenon of co-occurring events whose connection may have a deeper meaning even though their connection appears to be merely coincidental.

SYNTAX For any particular language, the rules governing the arrangement of words and allowing the meaning of the words to be understood.

T DATA Raymond Cattell's term for personality information gleaned from objective measures taken in experimental settings.

TEMPORAL CONTIGUITY In classical conditioning, as developed by Ivan Pavlov, a likely requirement for strong conditioning, involving the presentation of a conditioned stimulus (such as the striking of a tuning fork) immediately before the presentation of an unconditioned stimulus (such as meat powder).

THIRD FORCE A term used for humanistic psychology, which followed the so-called first (psychoanalysis) and second (behaviorism) forces in the historical development of psychology.

TOOLS OF INTELLECTUAL ADAPTATION Lev Vygotsky's term for the things that a culture instills in a child (such as language structures) that help the child think and learn.

TRACE CONDITIONING In classical conditioning, as developed by Ivan Pavlov, the result of inserting an interval of time between the presentation of a conditioned stimulus (such as the striking of a tuning fork) and the presentation of an unconditioned stimulus (such as meat powder).

TRANSFORMATIONAL GRAMMAR Noam Chomsky's term for his field of study, which has to do with language structure and with operations performed on sentences to create new sentences.

TRANSITIVITY The principle of relatedness among the parts of a series; in Jean Piaget's theory of child development, the child's understanding of this principle usually emerges during the concrete operational stage.

TRIAL AND ERROR A term association with Edward Thorndike's observation that learning occurs after repeated attempts and the gradual correction of mistakes.

UNCONDITIONAL POSITIVE REGARD In client-centered therapy, as developed by Carl Rogers, the therapist's warm and welcoming acceptance of the client.

UNCONDITIONED STIMULUS In classical conditioning, as developed by Ivan Pavlov, a stimulus (such as the presentation of meat powder) that automatically and naturally evokes a response (such as salivation).

UNCONSCIOUS MIND In psychoanalytic theory, as developed by Sigmund Freud, the area of the psyche that lies outside conscious awareness but can nevertheless drive behavior.

ZONE OF PROXIMAL DEVELOPMENT Lev Vygotsky's term for the gap between what a child can accomplish independently and what the child can accomplish with the guidance of a competent teacher; for Vygotsky, this gap is where true learning takes place.

References

Allport, G. W. (1968). *The Person in Psychology: Selected Essays*. Boston: Beacon Press.

Allport, G. W., & Odbert, H. S. (1936). Trait names: A psycholexical study. *Psychological Monographs, 47* (1, Whole No. 211).

American Psychiatric Association. (2013). *Diagnostic and Statistical Manual of Mental Disorders* (5th ed.). Arlington, VA: American Psychiatric Publishing.

Ansbacher, H. & Ansbacher, R. (Eds.) (1964). *The Individual Psychology of Alfred Adler: A Systematic Presentation in Selections from His Writings*. New York, NY: Harper Perennial.

Aronson, E. (2010). *Not by Chance Alone: My Life as a Social Psychologist*. New York, NY: Basic Books.

Aronson, E. (2011). *The Social Animal* (11th ed.) New York, NY: Worth/Freeman.

Aronson, E. Retrieved from www.jigsaw .org

Bandura, A. (1965). Influence of models' reinforcement contingencies on the acquisition of imitative responses. *Journal of Personality and Social Psychology, 1*(6), 589.

Bandura, A. (1977). *Social Learning Theory*. Englewood Cliffs, NJ: Prentice Hall.

Bandura, A., Ross, D., & Ross, S.A. (1961). Transmission of aggression through imitation of aggressive models. *Journal of Abnormal and Social Psychology, 63*, 575–82.

Bandura, A., Ross, D., & Ross, S. A. (1963). Imitation of film-mediated aggressive models. *The Journal of Abnormal and Social Psychology, 66*(1), 3.

Barlow, D. H. and V. Mark Durand. *Abnormal Psychology: An Integrative Approach*. (7th ed.) New York, NY: Cengage Learning.

Beck, A. T. (1967). *Depression: Causes and Treatment*. Philadelphia, PA: University of Pennsylvania Press.

Beck, A. T., Epstein, N., & Harrison, R. (1983). Cognitions, attitudes and personality dimensions in depression. *British Journal of Cognitive Psychotherapy 1*, 1–16.

Beck, A. T, & Steer, R. A. (1993). *Beck Anxiety Inventory Manual*. San Antonio, TX: Harcourt Brace and Company.

"Button, Button." *The Twilight Zone*. CBS. March 7, 1986. (Television.)

Cattell, R. B. (1957). *Personality and Motivation: Structure and Measurement*. New York, NY: World.

Cattell, R. B. (1963). Theory of crutallized intelligence: A critical experiment. *Journal of Educational Psychology*, 54, 1–22.

Chomsky, N. (1957). *Syntactic Structures*. The Hague, Netherlands.

Darwin, C. (1874). *The Descent of Man, and Selection in Relation to Sex* (2nd ed). New York, NY: A. L. Burt.

Darwin, C. (1958). *The Origin of Species, by Means of Nautral Selection or the Preservation of Favoured Races in the Struggle for Life*. New York, NY: New American Library. (Original work published 1859.)

Darwin, C. (1979). *The Expression of Emotions in Man and Animals*. London, UK: Julian Friedmann. (Original work published 1872.)

Dobkin, M. (January 16, 2006). Behaviorists behaving badly. *New York Magazine*.

Dweck, C. S. (1999). *Self-Theories: Their Role in Motivation, Personality and Development*. Philadelphia, PA: Psychology Press.

Dweck, C. S. (2006). *Mindset: The New Psychology of Success*. New York, NY: Random House.

Ellis, A. (1954). *The American Sexual Tragedy*. New York, NY: Twayne.

Ellis, A. (1957). Rational psychotherapy and individual psychology. *Journal of Individual Psychology*, *13*, 38–44.

Ellis, A. (1957). *How to Live with a Neurotic*. Oxford, UK: Crown.

Ellis, A. (1958). *Sex without Guilt*. New York, NY: Hillman.

Ellis, A. (1962). *Reason and Emotion in Psychotherapy*. New York, NY: Stuart.

Ellis, A. (1994). *Reason and Emotion in Psychotherapy*, Revised and Updated. Secaucus, NJ: Carol.

Erikson, E. (1950). *Childhood and Society*. New York, NY: W. W. Norton.

Erikson, E. (1968). *Identity: Youth and Crisis*. New York, NY: W. W. Norton Company.

Frankl, Viktor E. (1963–2007). *Man's Search for Meaning. An Introduction to Logotherapy*. Boston: Beacon Press. (A revised edition of *From Death-Camp to Existentialism*).

Gold, M. (Ed.). (1999). *A Kurt Lewin Reader: The Complete Social Scientist*. Washington, DC: American Psychological Association.

Haney, C., Banks, W. C., & Zimbardo, P. G. (1973). A study of prisoners and guards in a simulated prison. *Naval Research Review, 30*, 4–17.

Harlow, H. F. (1951). *Primate Learning*. In C. P. Stone (Ed.), *Comparitive Psychology* (183–238). Englewood Cliffs, NJ: Prentice-Hall.

Horney, K. (1942). *Self-Analysis*. New York, NY: W. W Norton.

Horney, K. (1945). *Our Inner Conflicts: A Constructive Theory of Neurosis*. New York, NY: W. W. Norton.

Horney, K. (1950). *Neurosis and Human Growth: The Struggle toward Self-realization*. New York, NY: W. W. Norton.

James, W. (1950). *The Principles of Psychology*. New York, NY: Dover Publications.

Jung, C. G. (1969). *The Collected Works of C.G. Jung*. Princeton, NJ: Princeton University. (Original work published 1948.)

Jung, C. G., Read, H., Fordham, M., & Adler, G. (1953). *The Collected Works of C. G. Jung*. New York, NY: Pantheon.

Lewin, K. (1947). Frontiers in group dynamics: Concept, method and reality in social science; social equilibria and social change. *Human Relations 1*, 36.

Loeschen, S. (1998). *Systematic Training in the Skills of Virginia Satir*. Pacific Grove, CA: Brooks/Cole.

Loftus, E. F. (1975). Leading questions and the eyewitness report. *Cognitive Psychology 7*, 560–572.

Loftus, E. F. (1979). The malleability of human memory. *American Scientist* 67, 312–320.

Loftus, E. F. (2007). Memory distortions: Problems solved and unsolved. In Garry, M. & Hayne, H. *Do justice and let the sky fall: Elizabeth F. Loftus and her contributions to science, law, and academic freedom*. (pp. 1–14.) Mahwah, NJ: Lawrence Erlbaum Associates.

Loftus, E. F., and Palmer, J. C. (1974). Reconstruction of automobile destruction: an example of the interaction between language and memory." *Journal of Verbal Learning and Verbal Behavior*, *13*, 585–589.

Maslow, A. H. (1943). A theory of human motivation. *Psychological Review,50*(4), 370–96.

Maslow, A. H. (1954). *Motivation and Personality*. New York, NY: Harper and Row.

Maslow, A. H. (1962). *Towards a Psychology of Being*. Princeton: D. Van Nostrand Comp.

Milgram, S. (1963). Behavioral study of obedience. *Journal of Abnormal and Social Psychology*, *67*(4): 371–378.

Milgram, S. (1967). The small world problem. *Psychology Today*.

Milgram, S. (1974). *Obedience to Authority*. New York, NY: Harper.

Neisser, U. (1982). *Memory Observed*. San Francisco, CA: Freeman.

Neisser, U. (1982). Snapshots or benchmarks? In U. Neisser & I. E. Hyman (Eds.), *Memory Observed: Remembering in Natural Contexts* (pp. 68–74). San Francisco, CA: Worth Publishers.

Neisser, U., & Harsch, N. (1992). Phantom flashbulbs: False recollections of hearing the news about Challenger. In E. Winograd & U. Neisser (Eds.), *Affect and Accuracy in Recall: Studies of "Flashbulb" Memories* (Vol. 4, pp. 9–31). New York, NY: Cambridge University.

Pavlov, I. P. (1955). *Selected Works*. Moscow, USSR: Foreign Languages Publishing House.

Piaget, J. (1952). *The Origins of Intelligence in Children*. New York, NY: International Universities Press.

Piaget, J. (1954). *The Construction of Reality in the Child* (M. Cook, Trans.).

Rogers, C. (1942). *Counseling and Psychotherapy*. New York, NY: Houghton Mifflin.

Rogers, C. (1951). *Client-Centered Therapy*. Houghton Mifflin Company.

Rogers, C. (1961). *On Becoming a Person*. New York, NY: Houghton Mifflin.

Rosenhan, D. (1973). On being sane in insane places. *Science: 179*, 250–258.

Sagan, C. (1979). *Broca's Brain*. New York, NY: Random House.

Satir, V. (1991). *The Satir Model: Family Therapy and Beyond*. Palo Alto, CA: Science and Behavior Books.

Schiller, F. (1983). Paul Broca and the history of aphasia. *Neurology 33*(5), 667.

Skinner, B. F. (1938). *The Behavior of Organisms*. New York, NY: Appleton-Centuty-Crofts.

Skinner, B. F. (1948). *Walden Two*. New York, NY: Macmillan.

Skinner, B. F. (1951). Some contributions of an experimental analysis of behavior to psychology as a whole. *American Psychologist*.

Skinner, B. F. (1953). *Science and Human Behavior*. New York, NY: Macmillan Company.

Skinner, B. F. (1957). *Schedules of reinforcement* (with C. B. Ferster). New York, NY: Appleton-Century-Crofts.

Skinner, B. F. (1963). Operant behavior. *American Psychologist, 18*, 503–515.

Skinner, B. F. (1971). *Beyond Freedom and Dignity*. New York, NY: Knopf.

Strachey, J. & Freud, A. (Eds.) (1953–1964). *The Standard Edition of the Complete Psychological Works of Sigmund Freud*, 24 vols. London, UK: W. W. Norton.

Thorndike, E. L. (1898). Animal intelligence: An experimental study of the associative processes in animals. *Psychological Monographs: General and Applied, 2*(4), i–109.

Thorne, B. M., & Henley, T. B. (2001). *Connections in the History and Systems of Psychology*. New York, NY: Houghton Mifflin.

Vygotsky, L. S. (1978). *Mind in Society: The Development of Higher Psychological Processes*. Cambridge, MA: Harvard.

Watson, J. (1913). Psychology as the behaviorist views it. *Psychological Review, 20*, 158–177.

Watson, J. (1928). *The Ways of Behaviorism*. New York, NY: Harper & Brothers.

Zimbardo, P. (2007). When Good People Do Evil. *Yale Alumni Magazine*.

Zimbardo, P. (2008, February). *Philip Zimbardo: The Psychology of Evil*. TED Talk [Video file.] Retrieved from https://www.ted.com/talks/philip_zimbardo_on_the_psychology_of_evil?language=en.

Index

Acknowledgments

Many thanks to my savvy and supportive literary agent, Linda Konner. Such a pleasure to work with you again, and on this new frontier! Elizabeth Castoria and the team at Callisto could not have been more energetic, wise, or supportive. Arthur Nazaryan's tireless and meticulous editing made me certain he slept as little as I did.

To my readers of Baggage Check, *The Friendship Fix*, and at *Psychology Today*, you've been with me for so many years now, and I simply wouldn't get to write if you didn't keep reading. I appreciate it more than you know. And my audiences, you keep paying attention—and even laughing when I hope you will—and I couldn't be more amazed or more honored that you let me keep talking.

My clients show me every week why the theories and research matter: you've trusted me with your secrets, your burdens, your pain, your joy, and ultimately, your lives. It's a tremendous privilege to be let in in this way, and I carry that with me always. My students over a decade have inspired and delighted me, teaching me so much in the process. Seeing you look at life in new ways, through the lens of psychological study, remains one of my greatest professional joys.

Utmost thanks to my wonderful research and teaching assistant, Nicole Conrad, a true gem. Thank you for making sure I didn't say things like "Charles Darwin, who was born in Kazakhstan……"

Boundless gratitude to my cheerleading section for what seemed like a "You're joking, right?" deadline: Heidi Brown, Monica Silvestro, my JE peeps who were not shy in reminding me of my legendarily quick term papers in college, the DCE, the "Brain Trust," and Laura Gertz. My first-ever editor Holly Morris continues to support and motivate me in innumerable ways more than a decade later, and my current Baggage Check editor Adam Sapiro provided a weekly dose of patience and sanity when my brain was fried during crunch time. I am bolstered by some tremendous people.

To my amazing family, far and wide: Mom, Dad, Greg, Jeff, Sybil, Luis, David, Judy, and beloved others, you are fantastic. To Andy, my utmost, and Vance, Alina, and Ruby—you are it. There's nothing bigger or greater any psychologist could imagine.

About the Author

ndrea Bonior, Ph.D., is a licensed clinical psychologist on the faculty of Georgetown University, and the longtime voice behind the mental health advice column "Baggage Check" in the *Washington Post Express*, which appears weekly in several newspapers nationwide. She also writes *Psychology Today*'s "Friendship 2.0" blog, and her expertise has appeared in media such as the *New York Times*, *USA Today*, *NPR*, *Forbes*, *Mic.com*, *Glamour*, *Self*, *MSNBC*, and *CNN*. Her first book, *The Friendship Fix*, explored how to maximize true friendship in the age of social media. She is a television contributor and speaker on relationships, work-life balance and mental health issues. She lives outside of Washington, DC, with her husband and three children. Join the discussion at her Facebook community, @Dr. Andrea Bonior.

CPSIA information can be obtained
at www.ICGtesting.com
Printed in the USA
LVHW071027141121
703289LV00021B/2711